MARCEL PROUST

REMEMBRANCE OF THINGS PAST

COMBRAY

Adaptation and Art:
Stéphane Heuet

Color:
Véronique Dorey

NBM ComicsLit

To Suzel, to my children Fleur Lise and Jean-Baptiste

Acknowledgments
La Société des Amis de Marcel Proust
et des Amis de Combray – Institut Marcel Proust International,
its President, Mr. Jean-Pierre Angremy, of the Académie française,
the President of the Bibltiothèque Nationale de France,
and its Secretary General, my friend Anne Borrel,
whose assistance and encouragement have been priceless,
M. Jean-Pierre Samoyault, Conservateur général du Patrimoine,
Administrateur général du Mobilier National
et des manufactures des Gobelins, de Beauvais et de la Savonnerie,
Mme. Michèle Pierron, librarian of the Musée de l'Armée,
Mme. Marie-Claude de Maneville, of the Société Nouvelle d'Exploitation de la Tour Eiffel,
Mme. Catherine Fajour, of Éditions Gallimard,
Messrs. Gérard Toupet and Guillaume Piens, of the Hôtel Scribe, first seat of the Jockey Club,
Mme. Brigitte Guillamot, of the Société Nancéienne Varin-Bernier,
The mayor and residents of Illiers-Combray (Eure-et-Loir),
and all the friends who helped me.

Bibliography
"Guide des maisons d'artistes et d'écrivains en région parisienne" – Dominique Camus (La Manufacture)
"Les Promenades de Marcel Proust" – Nadine Beauthéac-François-Xavier Bouchart (Éditions du Chêne)
"Marcel Proust" – Diane de Margerie (Christian Pirot)
"Proust, la cuisine retrouvée" – Anne Borel (Éditions du Chêne)
"Proust, par lui-même" – Claude Mauriac (Écrivains de toujours/ Seuil)

ISBN 1-56163-278-3 hc
ISBN 1-56163-289-9 pb
LC # 2001086437

Translated by Joe Johnson
Lettering by Michael Wood
Printed in Hong Kong

Comicslit is an imprint and
trademark of

NANTIER · BEALL · MINOUSTCHINE
Publishing inc.
new york

PART ONE

COMBRAY

For a long time, I would go to bed early.
...and when I would awaken in the middle of the night, since I was unaware of where I was, at first I did not even know who I was;
...but then the memory (not yet of the place where I was, but of some of those where I had lived and where I could have been) came to me like help from above to pull me away from the void...
...My memory was set in motion...
GRAND HOTEL
...I would spend the better part of the night remembering our past life at my great-aunt's in Combray, at Balbec, Paris, Doncières, Venice, and elsewhere still...

At Combray, everyday as the afternoon ended, long before the moment when I would have to go to bed and remain there, sleeplessly, far from my mother and grandmother, my bedroom would again become the painful, fixed point of my worries.
In order to distract me on evenings when I seemed too unhappy, someone had had the good idea to give me a magic lantern...
YOUR MOTHER TOLD ME TO SET UP THE MAGIC LANTERN WHILE WAITING FOR DINNER TIME.
YOUR GREAT-AUNT'S COMING UP.
I'VE PREPARED THE LEGEND OF GENEVIEVE DE BRABANT
VERY WELL, FRANCOISE
THIS EVENING WE'RE HAVING BEEF CASSEROLE.
"...SO THE WICKED GOLO GAVE THE ORDER TO HIS LACKEYS TO THROW THE POOR GENEVIEVE IN THE DUNGEON..."
"...MOVED BY SUCH MISFORTUNE, THE SWORDSMEN PRETENDED TO PUT HER TO DEATH AND LET HER FLEE INTO THE FOREST..."
"...FOR MONTHS, POOR GENEVIEVE HID WITH HER CHILD IN THE DEPTHS OF THE FOREST..."
"...FEARING THAT THE INFAMOUS GOLO WOULD FIND AND KILL HER..."

DING
DING
DING
DINNER'S SERVED!
After dinner, alas, I was soon obliged to leave Mama who would stay to chat with the others, in the garden if it were nice out, in the small parlor where everyone would retire if the weather were bad.
AH, IT'S RAINING.
FRANCOISE, SERVE THE LIQUEURS IN THE PARLOR.
Everyone, except my grandmother who, in all weather, even when the rain was pouring, would run up and down the soaked pathways.
IT'S A SHAME TO STAY SHUT AWAY IN THE COUNTRY. YOU CAN FINALLY BREATHE!
When these walks in the garden took place after dinner, only one thing had the power to draw her back inside:
To tease her, since my grandfather was forbidden any liqueurs, my great-aunt would make him drink a few drops.
GO AHEAD, AMADEE.
BATHILDE! COME STOP YOUR HUSBAND FROM DRINKING ANY BRANDY!
Alas! I was unaware that, far more than her husband's slight dietary slips, it was my own lack of will power, my delicate health, the uncertainty they cast on my future that sadly worried my grandmother during the course of those perambulations...

My sole consolation, when I would go upstairs to sleep, was that Mama would come up to kiss me once I was in my bed.
But this goodnight lasted for so little time...I got to where I hoped that it would come as late as possible, so the moment of respite when Mama had not yet come might be prolonged.
But on the whole, those evenings when my Mama spent so little time in my room,
were sweet indeed when compared to those when there were guests for dinner and when, because of that, she would not come up to say goodnight.
Our company was usually limited to Monsieur Swann, who, besides a few passing strangers, was about the only person who ever came to our house, sometimes for a neighborly dinner (less often since his unfortunate marriage, for my parents did not wish to welcome his wife), sometimes after dinner, just dropping in...
DING
DING.
A VISITOR? WHO COULD THAT BE?
DON'T WHISPER, NOTHING'S MORE UNPLEASANT FOR SOMEONE JUST ARRIVING.

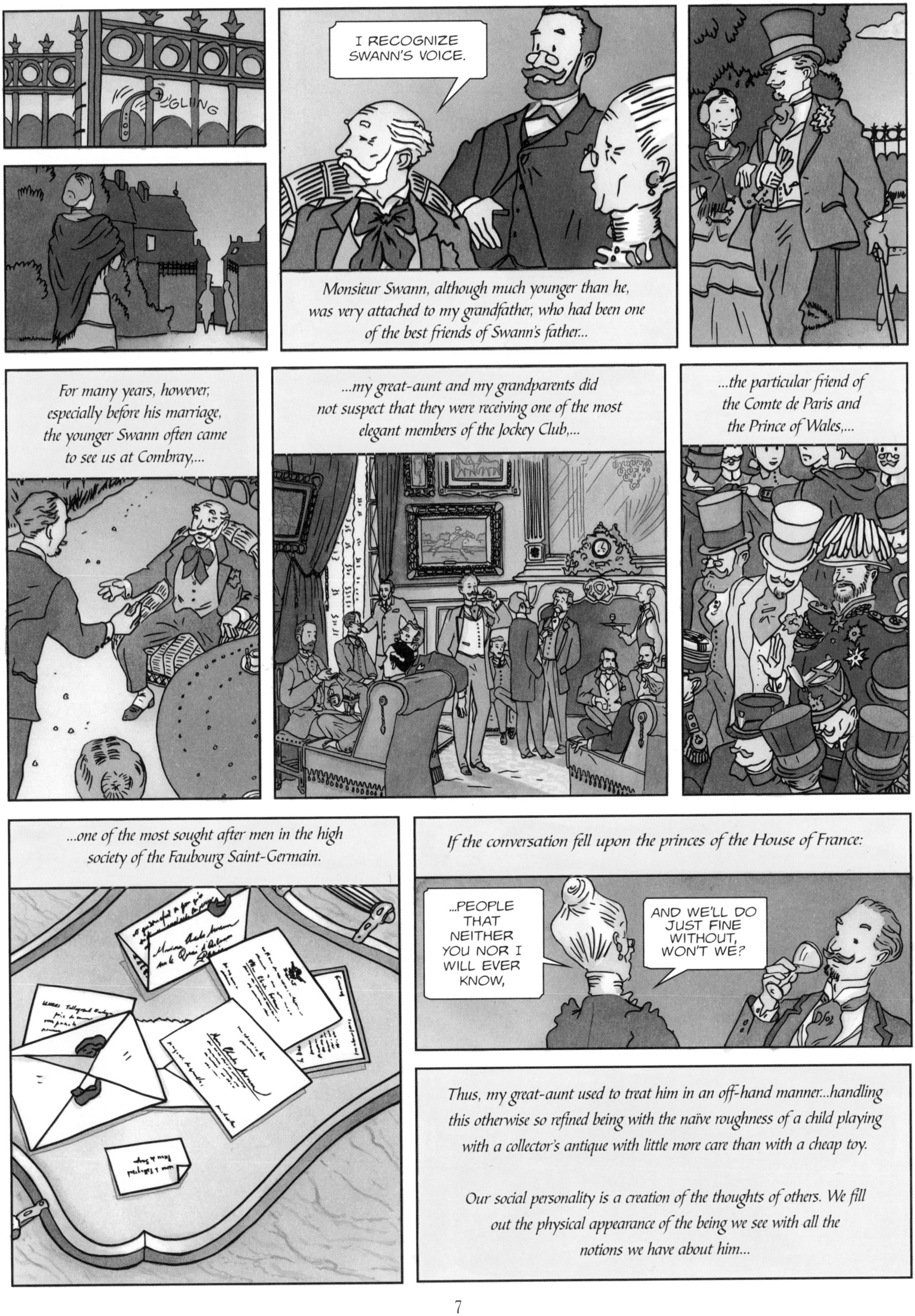
GLING
I RECOGNIZE SWANN'S VOICE.
Monsieur Swann, although much younger than he, was very attached to my grandfather, who had been one of the best friends of Swann's father...
For many years, however, especially before his marriage, the younger Swann often came to see us at Combray,...
...my great-aunt and my grandparents did not suspect that they were receiving one of the most elegant members of the Jockey Club,...
...the particular friend of the Comte de Paris and the Prince of Wales,...
...one of the most sought after men in the high society of the Faubourg Saint-Germain.
If the conversation fell upon the princes of the House of France:
...PEOPLE THAT NEITHER YOU NOR I WILL EVER KNOW,
AND WE'LL DO JUST FINE WITHOUT, WON'T WE?
Thus, my great-aunt used to treat him in an off-hand manner...handling this otherwise so refined being with the naïve roughness of a child playing with a collector's antique with little more care than with a cheap toy.
Our social personality is a creation of the thoughts of others. We fill out the physical appearance of the being we see with all the notions we have about him...

Middle-class people back then had a rather Hindu idea about society and considered it to be composed of closed castes where each individual, from his birth on, found himself placed into the rank his parents occupied, from which nothing could remove you...
...and allow you to climb to a superior caste.
MY GOODNESS! SWANN IS ONE OF THE MOST FAITHFUL REGULARS AT THE LUNCHES OF THE DUC DE ...
AMEDEE! PLEASE!
BUT AFTER ALL, SWANN COULD ASK HIM FOR ME WHY HIS UNCLE, IN HIS MEMOIRS...
AMEDEE, WHAT PLEASURE DO YOU FIND SPEAKING OF SUCH FOOLISHNESS?
FOOLISHNESS? PASQUIER? A PRESI-DENT OF THE HOUSE OF PEERS!
HOW UNBECOMING! A SWANN AT THE LUNCHES OF A DUKE!
POOR SWANN.
DID YOU SEE THAT HE'S ALSO "HONORED" IN LE FIGARO?
ONE OF THE PAINTINGS FROM HIS COLLECTION IS IN THE COROT EXHIBITION!
SINCE HE'S COMING TO DINNER TOMOR-ROW, WE'LL TALK TO HIM ABOUT IT
I DON'T THINK YOU'D PLEASE HIM AT ALL; I KNOW THAT IT WOULD BE QUITE UNPLEASANT FOR ME TO SEE MY NAME BOLDLY PRINTED LIKE THAT IN A NEWSPAPER, AND I WOULDN'T AT ALL BE FLAT-TERED IF SOMEONE TALKED TO ME ABOUT IT.
GOOD LORD, I'LL HAVE TO HAVE DINNER BEFORE EVERY-ONE ELSE TOMORROW,
AND MAMA WON'T COME UP TO KISS ME.

IT'S FROM MR. SWANN FOR MONSIEUR AMEDEE'S SISTERS-IN-LAW.
VINO DE ASTI
AND, THE EVENING OF THE DINNER...
DING DING
DO THINK TO THANK HIM INTELLIGIBLY FOR HIS WINE, YOU KNOW HOW DELICIOUS IT IS AND THE CASE IS ENORMOUS.
DON'T START WHISPERING,
HOW PLEASANT IT IS TO ARRIVE IN A HOUSE WHERE EVERYONE'S SPEAKING IN HUSHED TONES!
COME ALONG AND SIT WITH ALL OF US!
...AND WHAT DOES AUDIFFRET-PASQUIER HAVE TO SAY, SINCE IT SEEMS THAT YOU DINE WITH HIM?
I SAY. WHAT I AM GOING TO TELL YOU HAS MORE TO DO WITH WHAT YOU'RE ASKING ME THAN IT MAY APPEAR. I WAS...
I MET A RATHER KIND NEIGHBOR OF MONSIEUR VINTEUIL.
MONSIEUR VINTEUIL ISN'T THE ONLY ONE TO HAVE KIND NEIGHBORS!
?
...RIGHT, SO I WAS RE-READING SAINT-SIMON'S MEMOIRS THIS MORNING...
...IT'S SCARCELY MORE THAN A JOURNAL, BUT ADMIRABLY WRITTEN AND...
THERE ARE DAYS WHEN READING JOURNALISM SEEMS RATHER PLEASANT TO ME...
...WHEN THEY SPEAK OF THINGS AND PEOPLE WHO INTEREST US!
!
RIGHT...SO, SAINT-SIMON SAYS ABOUT MAULEVRIER: "NEVER DID I SEE IN THAT CRUDE BOTTLE ANYTHING OTHER THAN ILL-HUMOR, COARSENESS, AND FOOLISHNESS."
CRUDE OR NOT, I KNOW OF SOME BOTTLES WHERE THERE'S SOMETHING ELSE ALTOGETHER...

REMIND ME OF THE VERSE THAT YOU TAUGHT ME THAT ALWAYS COMFORTS ME IN SUCH MOMENTS. AH, YES: "LORD, HOW MUCH VIRTUOUSNESS YOU MAKE US HATE!"
THE LITTLE ONE LOOKS TIRED, HE SHOULD GO ON UP TO BED. BESIDES, WE'RE EATING LATER THIS EVENING.
YES, GO AHEAD, GET TO BED.
DINNER IS SERVED!
NO, NO, GO ON AND LET YOUR MOTHER BE, YOU'VE BOTH SAID GOODNIGHT ENOUGH, THESE DISPLAYS ARE RIDICULOUS. GET ON UPSTAIRS!
FRANCOISE, DID YOU SET UP THE SUMMER BED IN HIS ROOM?
YES, MA'AM, THE LITTLE IRON BED.

I wanted to try a condemned man's ruse...
Mama
I beg you come up and see me, it's very important
FRANCOISE, COULD YOU TAKE THIS NOTE TO MAMA?
WHILE THOSE LADIES AND GENTLEMEN ARE AT THE TABLE?
IT'S NOT MY FAULT! MAMA WANTED THIS ANSWER AND SHE'S AWAITING IT IMPATIENTLY!
Mama would surely come
WELL, I'LL GO SEE.
alas...
and later...
MADAME YOUR MOTHER SAYS TO TELL YOU THERE'S NO ANSWER.
DO YOU WANT SOME TEA, OR FOR ME TO STAY WITH YOU?
NO, THANK YOU, FRANCOISE, I'M GOING TO BED.
and I closed my eyes, trying not to hear the voices of my parents who were having coffee in the garden.

Suddenly...
NO! WHATEVER IT COSTS ME, I WON'T FALL ASLEEP WITHOUT SEEING MAMA AGAIN!
When my mother saw that I had stayed up to tell her goodnight again, they would enroll me to the school the next day
Oh, well!... I preferred that. What I wanted now was Mama and to tell her goodnight.
AH, THERE NOW, MONSIEUR SWANN HAS TAKEN HIS LEAVE.
...YES, THE CRAYFISH WAS GOOD, BUT THE ICE CREAM WAS RATHER ORDINARY.
WELL NOW! MY DEAR SISTERS-IN-LAW, YOU SEE, YOU DIDN'T THANK SWANN FOR THE ASTI...
WHAT, DIDN'T THANK HIM? I EVEN BELIEVE THAT I DID SO RATHER DELICATELY.
YES, YOU MANAGED THAT VERY WELL, AND I WAS RATHER PROUD OF MY BIT ABOUT THE KIND NEIGHBORS.
I THINK SWANN'S CHANGING. HE'S LIKE AN OLD MAN!
I THINK HE HAS A LOT OF WORRIES WITH THAT HUSSY OF A WIFE OF HIS WHO, AS ALL COMBRAY KNOWS, IS LIVING WITH A CERTAIN MONSIEUR DE CHARLUS.
WHAT, THAT'S WHAT YOU CALL THANKING! YOU CAN BE SURE THAT HE UNDERSTOOD NOTHING. I GIVE UP. I'M GOING TO BED.
?
RUN ALONG, RUN ALONG, SO AT LEAST YOUR FATHER DOESN'T SEE YOU LIKE THIS, WAITING LIKE A CRAZY BOY!
SO HE'S NOT ASLEEP THEN?
THE CHILD LOOKS RATHER SAD!
COME, COME SAY GOOD NIGHT!
SINCE THERE ARE TWO BEDS IN HIS ROOM, THEN SPEND THE NIGHT WITH HIM. ANYHOW, GOOD NIGHT. I'M NOT SO FRETFUL, SO I'M GOING TO BED.
!
!

Mama stayed in my bedroom that night. I ought to have been happy, but I was not.
It seemed to me that even if I had just won a victory, it was against her, and that this evening was the beginning of an era and would remain a sad date.
So it was for a long time, when, lying awake at night, recalling Combray, I never saw more than that kind of luminous image, cut out of indistinct shadows.
As if Combray had consisted of no more than two floors linked by a slender stairway, and as if it had never been but seven in the evening.
I would never have had any desire to dream of other things and other hours at Combray. All that was, in reality, dead to me.
Forever dead? Possibly.
It is wasted effort to seek to evoke our past. All the efforts of our intelligence are useless. It is hidden beyond the intellect's domain and reach, in some material object that we do not suspect.
It depends on happenstance that we come upon that object before our death, or that we do not.

For so many years, everything about Combray that was not the theatre and drama of my bedtime no longer existed for me, when...
IT'S HERE, COACHMAN, NUMBER 45.
YES, MONSIEUR.
MY POOR DEAR, YOU'RE FREEZING! FELICIE! MAKE US SOME TEA!
MAMA, YOU KNOW I NEVER DRINK TEA.
IT'LL WARM YOU UP. COME HAVE A SEAT.

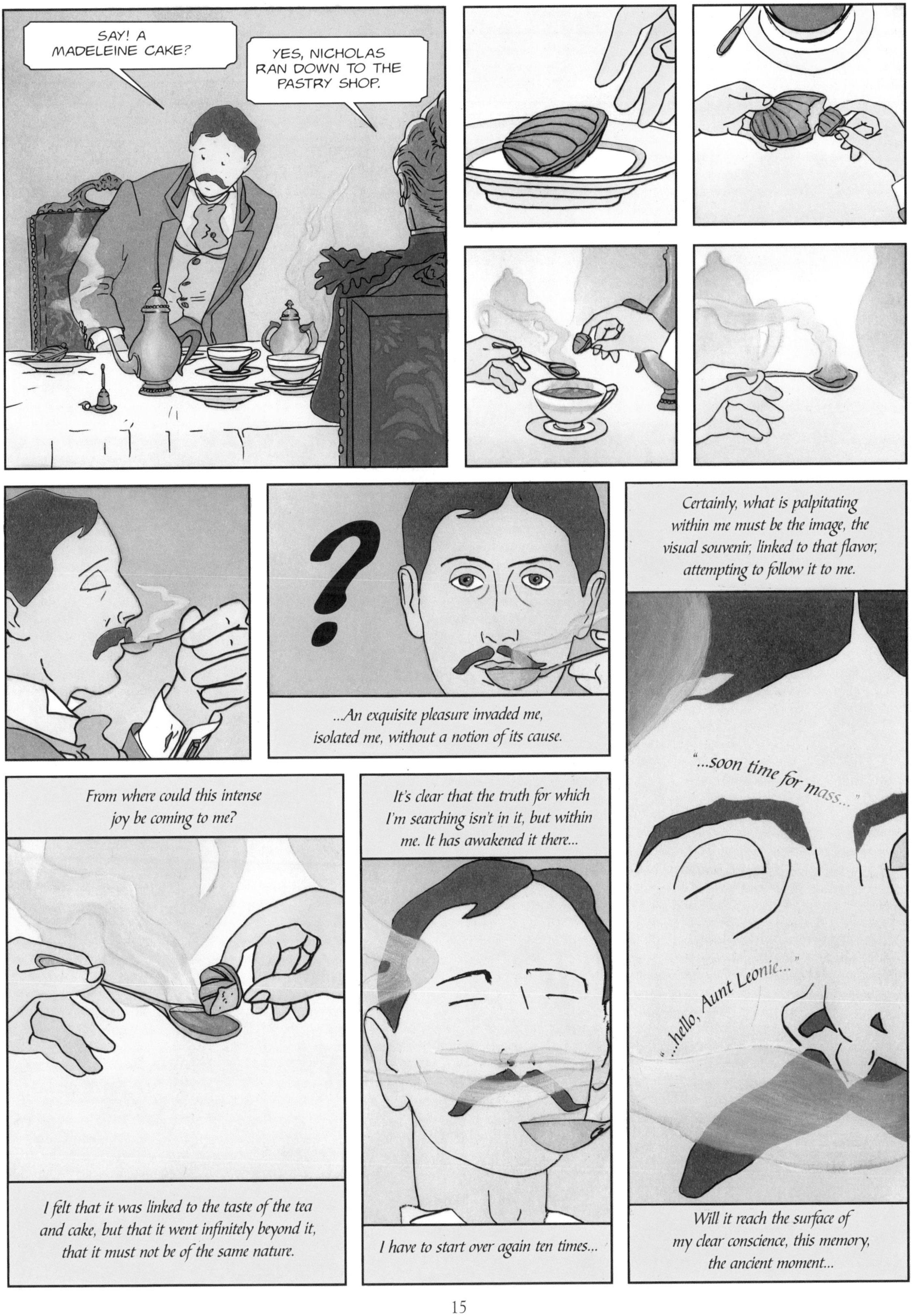

SAY! A MADELEINE CAKE?
YES, NICHOLAS RAN DOWN TO THE PASTRY SHOP.
...An exquisite pleasure invaded me, isolated me, without a notion of its cause.
Certainly, what is palpitating within me must be the image, the visual souvenir, linked to that flavor, attempting to follow it to me.
"...soon time for mass..."
"...hello, Aunt Leonie..."
From where could this intense joy be coming to me?
I felt that it was linked to the taste of the tea and cake, but that it went infinitely beyond it, that it must not be of the same nature.
It's clear that the truth for which I'm searching isn't in it, but within me. It has awakened it there...
I have to start over again ten times...
Will it reach the surface of my clear conscience, this memory, the ancient moment...

And suddenly the memory appeared to me.
"...hello, Aunt Leonie..."
That taste, it was the same as the little bit of madeleine that, on Sunday mornings at Combray, my aunt Léonie would give me after dipping it in her cup of tea or lime tea...
HELLO AUNT LEONIE!
...And, as in that game where the Japanese amuse themselves by steeping in a water-filled porcelain bowl small bits of paper until then indistinct which, scarcely dipped, stretch out and bend, take on color, differentiate themselves, becoming flowers, houses, people, substantial and
MARCHE
PATISSERIE
GRAINS-TOURTEAUX-ENGRAIS
QUINCAILLERIE
CHAUSSURE
AU COURS DES HALLES

recognizable, similarly now, all the flowers of our garden and those of Mr. Swann's park, and the water-lillies of the Vivonne, and the good folk of the village and their little dwellings and the church and all Combray and its surroundings, everything taking form and solidity, has emerged, city and gardens, from my cup of tea.

Combray was a little sad to live there, like its streets: Rue Saint-Hilaire, Rue Saint-Jacques where my aunt's house was...
MAMA, I'M GOING UP TO KISS AUNT LEONIE GOODBYE BEFORE MASS.
TOC
TOC
...my great aunt, with whom we lived, was the mother of that Aunt Léonie who, since the death of her husband, my Uncle Octave, had no longer wished to leave, first Combray, then her house, then her bedroom...
YOU CAN GO IN NOW, MADAME OCTAVE WILL SEE YOU.
...then her bed. She no longer "came down," always abed in a vague state of chagrin, of physical exhaustion, of sickness,...
HERE, YOUR LITTLE BIT OF MADELEINE.
VICHY
...of obsession, and of religious devotion.
GO ON, MY POOR DEAR, GO ON, GO GET READY FOR MASS; AND IF YOU RUN INTO FRANCOISE DOWN-STAIRS, TELL HER TO NOT BE TOO LONG ENJOYING HERSELF WITH YOU AND TO COME UP SOON TO SEE IF I NEED ANYTHING.
My aunt was resigned to depriving herself of Françoise to some extent during our stay.
She had the street within sight and read there, from morning till night, to relieve her boredom, in the fashion of Persian princes, the daily, but immemorial chronicle of Combray, which she would then discuss with Françoise.
FRANCOISE, MADAME GOUPIL WAS SO LATE FOR MASS, I WOULDN'T BE SURPRISED IF SHE ARRIVES AFTER THE ELEVATION.
OH! THAT SHOULDN'T COME AS ANY SURPRISE!
FRANCOISE, MADAME IMBERT'S JUST NOW GOING BY WITH ASPARAGUS TWICE AS BIG AS MOTHER CALLOT'S. SINCE YOU'VE BEEN PUTTING ASPARAGUS IN EVERY SAUCE THIS YEAR, ASK HER CLEANING WOMAN ABOUT THEM...
I'D NOT BE SURPRISED IF THEY WEREN'T FROM THE PRIEST'S.
AH, FROM THE PRIEST'S, I DO BELIEVE YOU, MY POOR FRANCOISE. I TELL YOU THAT THOSE WERE AS BIG AS AN ARM. NOT YOURS, OF COURSE, BUT LIKE MY OWN POOR ARM, WHICH HAS SHRUNKEN AGAIN SO THIS YEAR.
FRANCOISE, FOR WHOM DID THEY TOLL THE FUNERAL BELL? AH! MY LORD, IT MUST HAVE BEEN FOR MADAME ROUSSEAU WHO PASSED AWAY THE OTHER NIGHT. AH! IT'S TIME FOR THE GOOD LORD TO CALL ME HOME, I'VE LOST MY MIND. BUT I'M WASTING YOUR TIME, MY DEAR.
WHY NO, MADAME OCTAVE, MY TIME ISN'T SO DEAR; THE ONE WHO MADE IT DIDN'T SELL IT TO US.

Sometimes, these events took on such a mysterious and grave character that my aunt...
DING DING
DING DING
BUT, MADAME OCTAVE, IT'S NOT YET TIME FOR YOUR PEPSIN! ARE YOU FEELING FAINT?
NO, FRANCOISE, WELL, MAYBE... DON'T YOU KNOW I JUST SAW MME. GOUPIL WITH A LITTLE GIRL THAT I DIDN'T RECOGNIZE...
WHY THAT'S MONSIEUR PUPIN'S DAUGHTER.
OH! I DO BELIEVE YOU, BUT I WOULD HAVE RECOGNIZED HER!
BUT, I DON'T MEAN THE OLDER ONE, MADAME OCTAVE, I MEAN THE KID, THE ONE WHO'S IN THE JOUY BOARDING SCHOOL. IT SEEMS TO ME THAT I ALREADY SAW HER THIS MORNING.
AH! THAT MUST BE IT. SHE'LL HAVE COME FOR THE EASTER BREAK. THAT'S IT!
MY POOR FRANCOISE, I'VE MADE YOU COME UP FOR NOTHING.
But my aunt knew that it wasn't for "nothing"... for in Combray, someone "that nobody knew" was a creature as unbelievable as a god from mythology. We knew everybody so well in Combray, both animals and people, that if my aunt had by chance seen a dog pass by "that she didn't at all recognize," she would dwell on it ceaselessly...
THAT'LL BE MADAME SAZERAT'S DOG...
AS IF I DIDN'T KNOW MADAME SAZERAT'S DOG!
AH, IT'LL BE MONSIEUR GALOPIN'S DOG.
AH, IF THAT'S THE CASE.
IT SEEMS IT'S A RATHER FRIENDLY DOG.
MADAME OCTAVE, I'VE GOT TO GO, MY OVEN'S NOT EVEN LIT YET AND I STILL HAVE TO CLEAN THE ASPARAGUS.
WHAT, FRANCOISE, MORE ASPARAGUS!
YOU'VE GOT A REAL OBSESSION FOR ASPARAGUS THIS YEAR; YOU'RE GOING TO MAKE OUR PARISIANS TIRED OF THEM!
WHY NO, MADAME OCTAVE, THEY LIKE THEM. AND YOU'LL SEE HOW HEARTILY THEY'LL EAT THEM AFTER RETURNING FROM CHURCH.

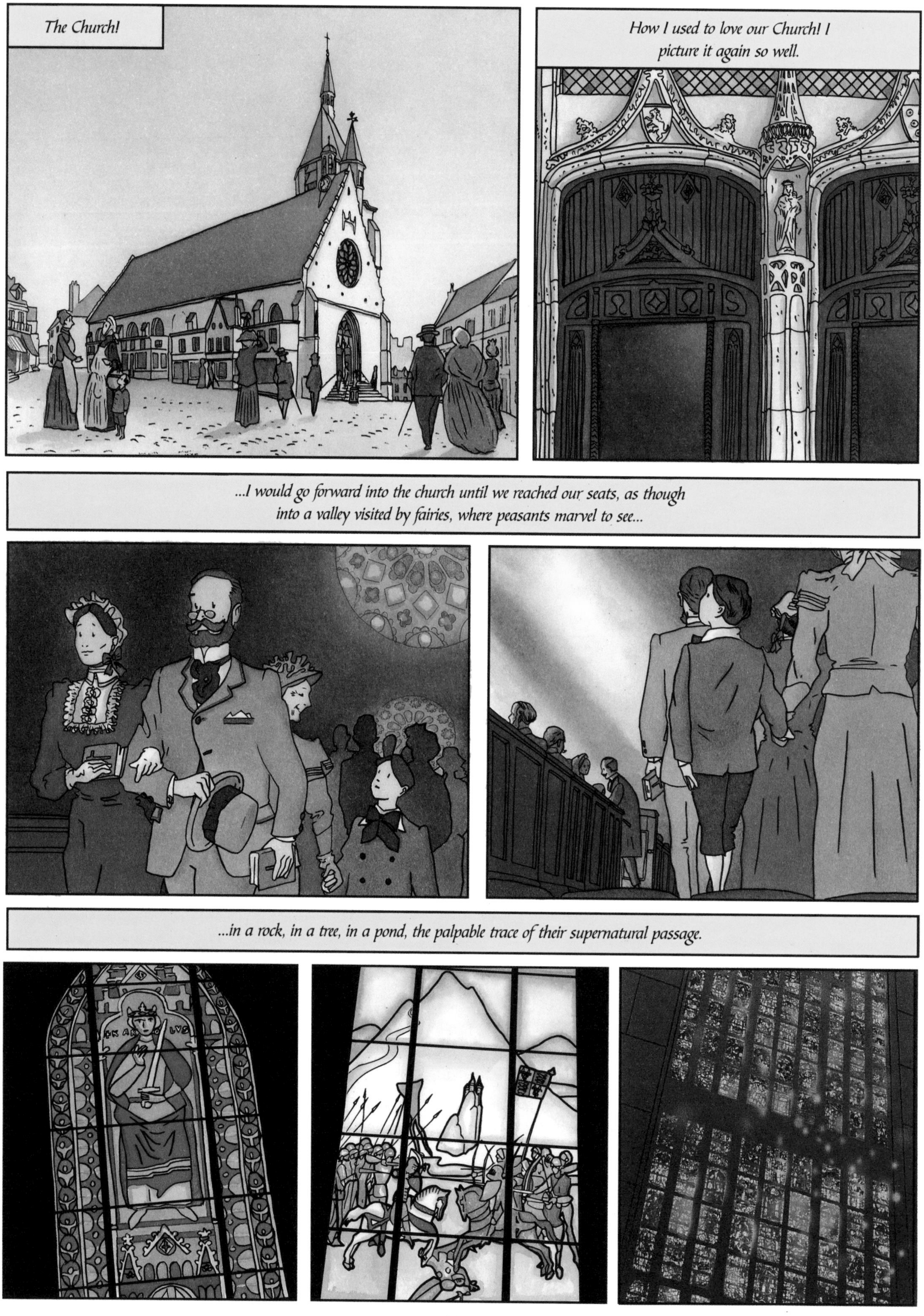
The Church!
How I used to love our Church! I picture it again so well.
...I would go forward into the church until we reached our seats, as though into a valley visited by fairies, where peasants marvel to see...
...in a rock, in a tree, in a pond, the palpable trace of their supernatural passage.

For me, all this made the church something entirely different from the rest of the town: a building occupying, if one can say so, a space of four dimensions—-the fourth being Time—-, a vessel sailing across the centuries, which, from bay to bay, from chapel to chapel, seemed to vanquish and stretch over, not merely the space of some yards, but the successive epochs from which it emerged victorious.
DONG
DONG
DONG

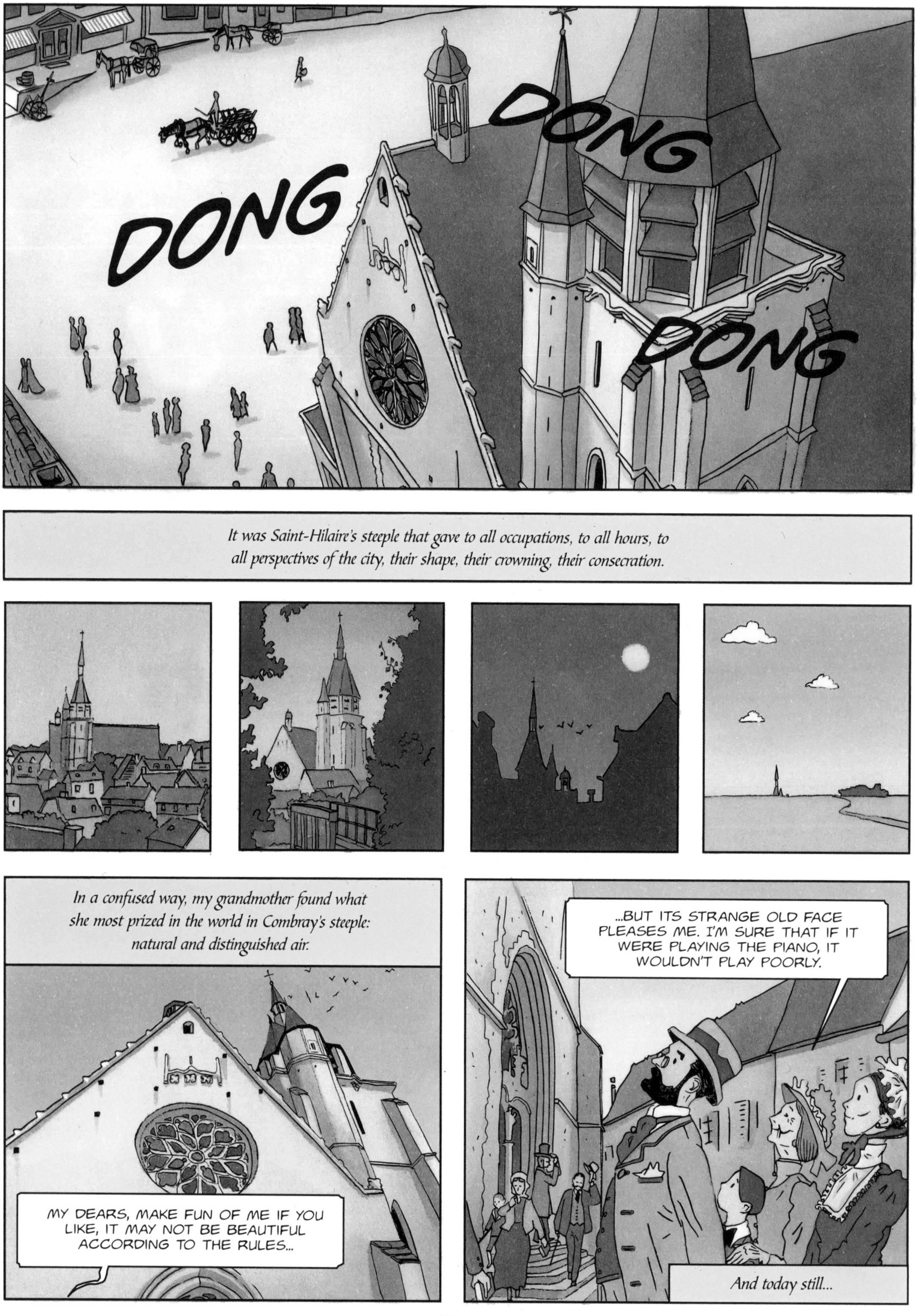
DONG
DONG
DONG
It was Saint-Hilaire's steeple that gave to all occupations, to all hours, to all perspectives of the city, their shape, their crowning, their consecration.
In a confused way, my grandmother found what she most prized in the world in Combray's steeple: natural and distinguished air.
MY DEARS, MAKE FUN OF ME IF YOU LIKE, IT MAY NOT BE BEAUTIFUL ACCORDING TO THE RULES...
...BUT ITS STRANGE OLD FACE PLEASES ME. I'M SURE THAT IF IT WERE PLAYING THE PIANO, IT WOULDN'T PLAY POORLY.
And today still...

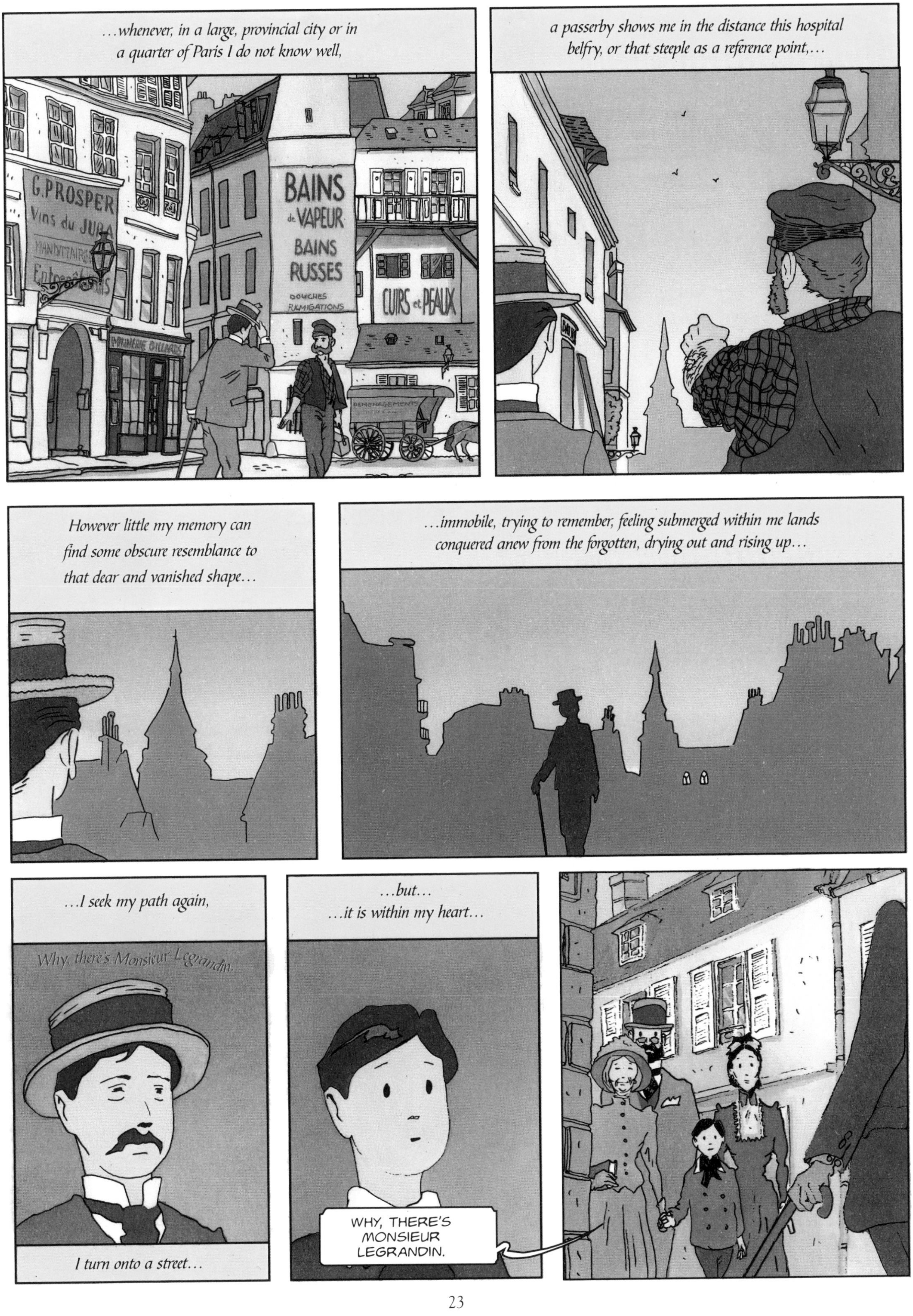
...whenever, in a large, provincial city or in a quarter of Paris I do not know well,
G. PROSPER
Vins du JURA
BAINS de VAPEUR
BAINS RUSSES
DOUCHES FUMIGATIONS
CUIRS et PEAUX
a passerby shows me in the distance this hospital belfry, or that steeple as a reference point,...
However little my memory can find some obscure resemblance to that dear and vanished shape...
...immobile, trying to remember, feeling submerged within me lands conquered anew from the forgotten, drying out and rising up...
...I seek my path again,
Why, there's Monsieur Legrandin.
I turn onto a street...
...but...
...it is within my heart...
WHY, THERE'S MONSIEUR LEGRANDIN.

Detained in Paris by his engineering profession, Monsieur Legrandin could, excepting long vacations, come to his property in Combray only from Saturday evening through Monday morning.
GREETINGS, FRIENDS!
He was one of those men who, in addition to a scientific career in which they have, moreover, brilliantly succeeded, possess an altogether different, literary, artistic culture, useless in their professional specialty, but by which their conversation profits.
TOMORROW I'LL HAVE TO GET BACK TO MY NICHE IN PARIS.
OH, THE ONLY NECESSITY LACKING THERE IS A BIG CHUNK OF SKY LIKE HERE!
My grandmother's only criticism of him was that he spoke a little too well, a little too much like a book.
She was also astonished at the inflammatory tirades he often unleashed against the aristocracy, at high society, and snobbery…
CERTAINLY, THAT'S THE SIN OF WHICH SAINT PAUL WAS THINKING WHEN HE SPEAKS OF THE SIN FOR WHICH THERE'S NO FORGIVENESS.
Also, she did not find it in good taste that M. Legrandin, whose sister lived nearby, married to a gentleman of Lower Normandy, should give himself over to such violent attacks against the nobles…
THE REVOLUTION OUGHT TO HAVE GUILLOTINED THEM ALL!
STRIVE TO KEEP ALWAYS A BIT OF SKY OVER YOUR LIFE, CHILD!
MADAME OCTAVE'S WAITING FOR YOU IN HER ROOM, MADAME.
YES, FRANCOISE, WE'RE GOING UP.
YOU HAVE A LOVELY SOUL, OF A RARE QUALITY, AN ARTIST'S NATURE, DON'T LET IT LACK FOR WHAT IT NEEDS.

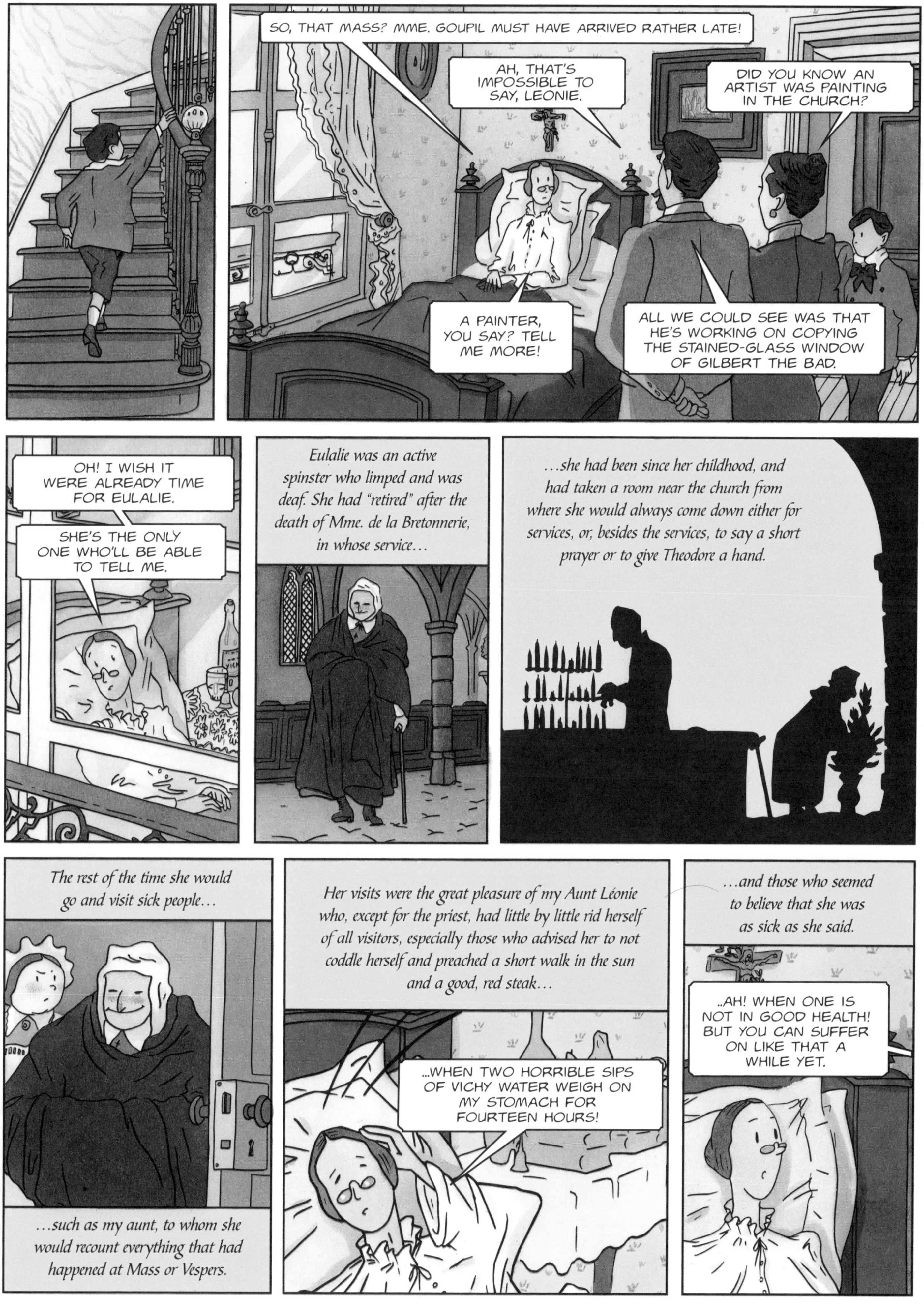
SO, THAT MASS? MME. GOUPIL MUST HAVE ARRIVED RATHER LATE!
AH, THAT'S IMPOSSIBLE TO SAY, LEONIE.
DID YOU KNOW AN ARTIST WAS PAINTING IN THE CHURCH?
A PAINTER, YOU SAY? TELL ME MORE!
ALL WE COULD SEE WAS THAT HE'S WORKING ON COPYING THE STAINED-GLASS WINDOW OF GILBERT THE BAD.
OH! I WISH IT WERE ALREADY TIME FOR EULALIE.
SHE'S THE ONLY ONE WHO'LL BE ABLE TO TELL ME.
Eulalie was an active spinster who limped and was deaf. She had "retired" after the death of Mme. de la Bretonnerie, in whose service…
…she had been since her childhood, and had taken a room near the church from where she would always come down either for services, or, besides the services, to say a short prayer or to give Theodore a hand.
The rest of the time she would go and visit sick people…
…such as my aunt, to whom she would recount everything that had happened at Mass or Vespers.
Her visits were the great pleasure of my Aunt Léonie who, except for the priest, had little by little rid herself of all visitors, especially those who advised her to not coddle herself and preached a short walk in the sun and a good, red steak…
…WHEN TWO HORRIBLE SIPS OF VICHY WATER WEIGH ON MY STOMACH FOR FOURTEEN HOURS!
…and those who seemed to believe that she was as sick as she said.
..AH! WHEN ONE IS NOT IN GOOD HEALTH! BUT YOU CAN SUFFER ON LIKE THAT A WHILE YET.

In a nutshell, my aunt demanded that everyone approve of her conduct, pity her for her suffering, and reassure her concerning her future.
Eulalie excelled in this…
IT'S THE END, MY POOR EULALIE.
KNOWING YOUR ILLNESS AS YOU DO, MADAME OCTAVE, YOU'LL MAKE IT TO A HUNDRED, AS MME. SAZERIN WAS TELLING ME JUST YESTERDAY.
SAZERAT, EULALIE, SAZERAT.
Her visits, which took place every Sunday, were for my aunt a pleasure the prospect of which kept her in an agreeable state…
IT'S SUNDAY, EULALIE WON'T BE LONG COMING.
But when too prolonged, this delight in waiting turned into torture…
ELEVEN O'CLOCK, AND EULALIE'S NOT YET COME!
On Sundays, she thought only of this visit,
YOU RANG, MADAME OCTAVE?
FRANCOISE, I FEEL… FAINT… UH… STILL NO EULALIE?
VICHY
as soon as lunch was over, Françoise hurried us to leave the dining room so she could go upstairs and keep my aunt "occupied."
But (especially once the good weather set in) the high hour of noon had long since passed around the table where we were still seated when…
LORD, I CAN'T TAKE IT ANY LONGER, WE'VE BEEN SITTING AT THIS TABLE FOR TWO HOURS! AND THIS HEAT…

Our menu reflected somewhat the rhythm of the seasons and incidents of life, for, upon a permanent foundation of eggs, cutlets, potatoes, preserves, and cookies, which she no longer even announced to us, Françoise would add, depending on the labors of the fields and orchards, the catch from the tide, the bargains in shops, the kindness of neighbors, and her own genius:
THE FISHWIFE GUARANTEED ITS FRESHNESS TO ME!
IT LOOKED LIKE A REAL BEAUTY TO ME AT THE ROUSSAINVILLE MARKET.
WHY, FRESH AIR MAKES ONE HUNGRY, NO?
I'VE NEVER BEFORE MADE YOU ANY CARDOONS WITH MARROW!
AT THIS TIME OF THE YEAR, THEY'RE STILL PRETTY SCARCE, YOU KNOW!
SPINACH WILL MAKE A NICE CHANGE...
MONSIEUR SWANN ESPECIALLY CAME BY TO DROP OFF THESE RASPBERRIES FOR YOU.
AH, THERE WON'T BE ANY MORE CURRANTS IN TWO WEEKS!
THE CHILD LOVES THAT SO MUCH!
JUST FIGURE, TWO YEARS AFTER THE CHERRY TREE WAS NO LONGER BEARING!
I ORDERED IT YESTERDAY.
IT'S OUR TURN TO OFFER ONE.
...AND TO TOP IT OFF, ESPECIALLY FOR MADAME'S HUSBAND...
CHO-CO-LATE CREAM!
NO NEED TO BE HUNGRY TO EAT THAT!
COME NOW, DON'T STAY HERE ALL DAY, GO UP TO YOUR ROOM IF IT'S TOO HOT FOR YOU OUTSIDE, BUT FIRST GO GET SOME FRESH AIR FOR A MOMENT SO YOU DON'T START READING RIGHT AFTER LEAVING THE TABLE.

In past times, before going up to read, I would go into the little sitting-room…
…that my uncle Adolphe, my grandfather's brother, who had retired as a major, used to occupy on the ground floor, and which always exuded that obscure, fresh, both woodsy and old-fashioned scent that makes your nostrils dream at length when you enter certain abandoned hunting lodges.
But I'd no longer been going to my Uncle Adolphe's room for a number of years. He no longer came to Combray because of a quarrel that had taken place between him and my family, through my fault, in the following circumstances:

Once or twice a month in Paris, I was sent to visit him while he was finishing his lunch.
MADELEINE
à la MADELEINE
SOIERIES
AH, YOU HAVEN'T BEEN OVER IN A WHILE! YOU'VE REALLY BEEN NEGLECTING ME. COME, CHILD, PICK OUT A MANDARIN ORANGE OR SOME MARZIPAN.
I'LL HAVE SOME COFFEE IN MY OFFICE.
YES, MAJOR.
We would stay there until:
MAJOR, THE COACHMAN ASKS WHEN HE SHOULD READY THE CARRIAGE.
...
A QUARTER PAST TWO.
A QUARTER PAST TWO? FINE...I'LL GO TELL HIM...
His answer was always, and infallibly, "a quarter past two."
Back then, I was smitten with the theatre, without ever having been there.
SPECTACLES
CIRQUE D'HIVER
CENDRILLON
L'HOMME OBUS
COMÉDIE FR
RACINE
PHÈDRE
SARAH BERN
LUCIEN GU
All of my conversations with my playmates were about actors: the Gots, the Delauneys, the Febvres, the Thirons, and Maubant, and Coquelin…
But if the actors preoccupied me so, how the view of a woman I thought to be an actress would leave me disturbed even longer!
I classified the most illustrious in order of talent: Sarah Bernhardt, Berma, Bartet, Madeleine Brohan, Jeanne Samary. And my uncle knew many of them…
…and also some tarts, whom I didn't clearly distinguish from the actresses.

And if we went to see him only on certain days, it was because on others women would come whom his family could not meet, at least in the family's opinion. For my uncle, on the contrary, his too great ease in paying pretty widows, who had perhaps never been married,…
…countesses with grandiose names,
…which no doubt were noms de guerre,
the compliment of introducing them to my grandmother
or even of giving them some family jewels,
had more than once gotten him into trouble with my grandfather.
Often, when the name of an actress came up in a conversation…
"A FRIEND OF YOUR UNCLE'S."
…I would think of the trial period that important men would undergo, for years perhaps, at the doorstep of the sort of woman who would not answer their letters. My uncle could have spared me this by introducing me at his home to the actress, unapproachable to so many others, yet who was his intimate friend.
Thus, under the pretext that a lesson had been rescheduled, one day other than the one reserved for the visits we paid him…
HA HA HA, DEAR FRIEND…
UH…WELL, YOUR UNCLE'S VERY BUSY!
I'LL GO SEE…
OH YES! DO LET HIM COME IN. IN THE PHOTOGRAPH, HE FAVORS YOUR NIECE SO MUCH. I'D LOVE TO SEE THE CHILD FOR JUST A MOMENT.

MY NEPHEW.
HE RESEMBLES HIS MOTHER SO!
BUT YOU'VE NEVER SEEN MY NIECE EXCEPT IN A PHOTOGRAPH...
I BEG YOUR PARDON, MY DEAR FRIEND, BUT I PASSED HER IN THE STAIRS LAST YEAR WHEN YOU WERE SO SICK.
HE TAKES AFTER HIS FATHER ESPECIALLY. HE'S JUST LIKE HIS FATHER AND ALSO MY POOR MOTHER.
I DON'T KNOW HIS FATHER AND I'VE NEVER MET YOUR POOR MOTHER, MY DEAR.
I was feeling a little disappointed. I found nothing of the theatrical aspect in her that I admired in the photographs of actresses, nor of the devilish expression that would have been in keeping with the life she supposedly led. I had trouble believing that she was a tart and would certainly not have believed her an elegant one if I had not seen the two-horse carriage, the pink dress, the pearl necklace,…
…if I had not known that my uncle only knew the very top of the line.
NO, DEAR, YOU KNOW I'M ACCUSTOMED TO THOSE THE GRAND DUKE SENDS ME. I TOLD HIM THEY MADE YOU JEALOUS.
WHY YES, I MUST HAVE MET THE FATHER OF THIS YOUNG MAN AT YOUR HOUSE. ISN'T HE YOUR NEPHEW? HOW COULD I HAVE FORGOTTEN? HE WAS SO NICE, SO DELIGHTFUL TO ME.
She had taken some insignificant comment by my father, had delicately refashioned it, …had rendered it into an artist's jewel, into something "altogether delightful."

Later it seemed to me that it was one of the most touching aspects of these idle, studious women's role, that they devote their generosity, their talent, a free dream of sentimental beauty, and a gold that costs them little, to embellish with a fine and precious setting the uncouth, rough-hewn life of men.
NOW LOOK HERE, IT'S TIME YOU GOT ON YOUR WAY.
GOOD LORD, HOW I WOULD LIKE TO KISS HER HAND!
SHOULD I DO SO OR SHOULD I NOT DO SO?
HOW SWEET HE IS! HE'S ALREADY GALLANT, HE'S A LITTLE LADY'S MAN...
...HE'S LIKE HIS UNCLE. HE'LL BE A PERFECT GENTLEMAN!
COULDN'T HE COME SOME TIME TO HAVE "A CUP OF TEA," AS OUR ENGLISH NEIGHBORS SAY?
HE'D ONLY NEED TO SEND ME A "BLUE" THAT MORNING...
WHY NO, THAT'S IMPOSSIBLE. HE'S VERY BUSY. HE STUDIES A LOT. HE WINS ALL THE SCHOOL PRIZES. WHO KNOWS? MAYBE HE'LL BE A LITTLE VICTOR HUGO, A SORT OF VAULABELLE, YOU KNOW!
I ADORE ARTISTS, THEY'RE THE ONLY ONES WHO UNDERSTAND WOMEN...
...THEM AND THE SELECT FEW LIKE YOURSELF.
UH,...CHILD, YOU'D BEST NOT SPEAK TO YOUR PARENTS OF THIS VISIT. IT WOULD HOLD NO INTEREST.
UNCLE ADOLPHE, BELIEVE ME, ONE DAY I'LL FIND A WAY TO THANK YOU.
THE MEMORY OF YOUR KINDNESS IS SO STRONG, SO STRONG...

It was so strong, in fact, that two hours later, I told my parents every little detail of the visit I had just made. I didn't imagine I would thus be causing my uncle any unpleasantness. How could I have thought so, since I didn't desire to do so?
My parents unfortunately, adopted entirely different principles than the ones I had suggested they adopt when they formed an opinion about my uncle's deed.
My father and grandfather had a violent argument with him...
I learned of it indirectly.
Several days later, passing my uncle outside... I felt the pain, gratitude, remorse I would have liked to express to him. In the face of their enormity, I thought that simply raising my hat would be petty. I resolved to abstain from this inadequate gesture and looked the other way.
My uncle thought that, by doing so, I was following my parents' orders. He did not forgive them and died many years later without any of us ever seeing him again.

So I no longer went into my Uncle Adolphe's now-closed sitting-room.
I'M GOING TO LET THE KITCHEN-GIRL SERVE THE COFFEE AND TAKE UP THE HOT WATER. I HAVE TO RUN ALONG TO MADAME OCTAVE'S.
The year when we ate so much asparagus, the kitchen-girl usually responsible for cleaning them was a poor, sickly creature, in a rather advanced state of pregnancy when we arrived at Easter, and we were even surprised that Françoise allowed her to do so many errands and tasks…
As Mr. Swann had made us notice, the folds of her ample smocks recalled the robes of some of the allegorical figures by Giotto.
HOW IS GIOTTO'S CHARITY?
She did, moreover, rather look like those strong and mannish virgins in whom the virtues are personified in the Chapel of the Arena.
And I now realize that those allegories of Virtues and Vices painted in the chapel in Padua resembled her in yet another respect:
Just as the image of this girl was enlarged by the added symbol she carried in her belly like an ordinary, heavy burden, without seeming to understand its meaning, without anything in her face betraying its beauty or spirit…
…so does the robust housewife represented in the Arena by the name of "Caritas" embody that virtue without seeming to have any suspicion of it, no thought of charity could ever seem to be expressed by her energetic, vulgar face.

For a long time, I took no pleasure in considering the copies of these figures by Giotto that Mr. Swann had brought to me. Charity without charity, Envy that looked like a plate in a medical book, Justice with the same grayish, meanly ordinary face as certain pretty, pious, dry bourgeoises in Combray…

KARITAS
...CHARITY HOLDING HER FLAMING HEART OUT TO GOD, "PASSING" IT TO HIM, RATHER, LIKE A COOKING WOMAN WOULD A CORKSCREW THROUGH THE BARS OF HER BASEMENT WINDOW...

...ENVY SEEMING TO ILLUSTRATE SOME COMPRESSION OF THE GLOTTIS OR THE UVULA BY A TUMOROUS TONGUE...

JUSTI CIA
...BOURGEOISES, SEVERAL OF WHOM HAD BEEN ALREADY ENLISTED IN INJUSTICE'S RESERVE MILITIAS...

...ANGER...

INFIDELITAS
...INFIDELITY...

...FICKLENESS...

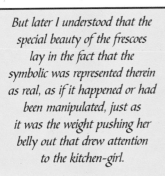

But later I understood that the special beauty of the frescoes lay in the fact that the symbolic was represented therein as real, as if it happened or had been manipulated, just as it was the weight pushing her belly out that drew attention to the kitchen-girl.

And perhaps this (at least apparent) non-participation of a being's soul in the virtue acting through them also has, beyond its esthetic virtue, a reality, if not psychological, then at least, as they say, physiognomic.

Later, when I had the occasion to meet truly saintly embodiments of active charity, they generally had the cheerful, positive, dispassionate, and brusque air of a busy surgeon, that face in which one cannot read any commiseration, any tenderness before human suffering, any fear of colliding with it, the antipathetic, sublime face devoid of gentleness that is the face of true goodness.

BLAM
BLAM
BLAM
BLAM
BZZZZZZZZ
BLAM
My sensation of the light's splendor was given to me solely by the blows struck on the Rue de la Cure…which, ringing in the sonorous atmosphere particular to hot weather, seemed to give far-away flight to scarlet stars…
YOU DID ASK ABOUT THE NOISE, EH?
WHY YES, CAMUS, FRANCOISE SAID YOU COULD SINCE MADAME OCTAVE ISN'T RESTING.
BLAM
BZZZZZZZ
BZZZZZZ
BZZ
BZZZZZZZZZ
...and also by the flies that were performing for me, in their own little concert, like music in a summer room.
B ZZ ZZ ZZ ZZ ZZ ZZ
BLAM
BLAM
That dim freshness in my room was to the street's broad daylight what shade is to a sunbeam, that is to say, just as luminous as it, and offered to my imagination the total spectacle of the summer, which my senses, if I have been on a stroll, could have enjoyed only in bits and pieces….
…and thus it was quite harmonious with my repose, which tolerated (thanks to the adventures recounted by my books) the shock and animation of a torrent of activity, similar to the repose of an immobile hand in the midst of running water.
OH, YOU'RE STILL ENJOYING YOUR READING! GO DOWN FOR A BIT OF FRESH AIR IN THE GARDEN!
Unwilling to give up my reading, I was at least going to continue it in the garden, in a small sentry-box…
…inside of which I would sit, thinking myself hidden…Were not my very thoughts also like another shelter deep within which I felt I remained buried, even to watch what was going on outside?

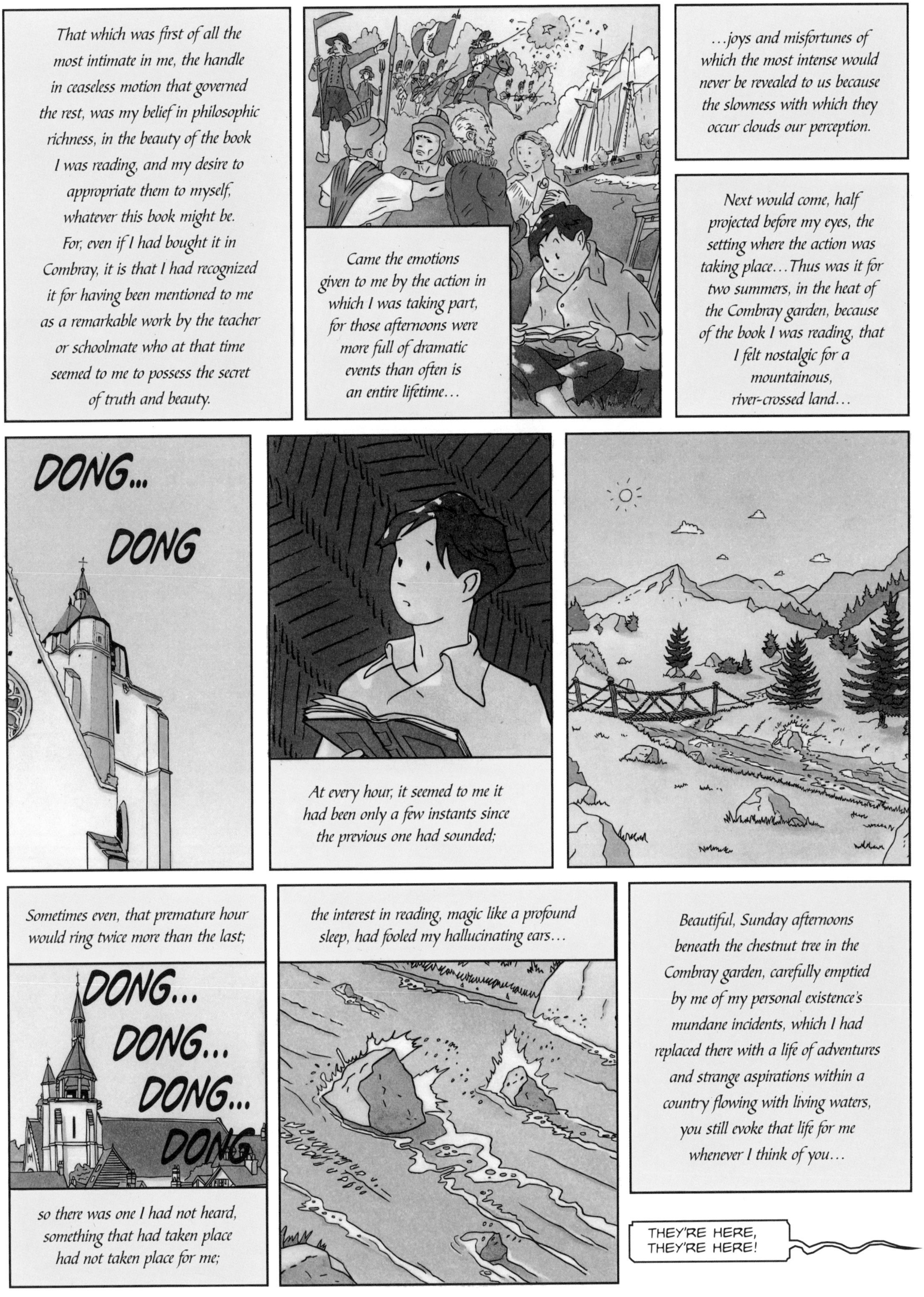
That which was first of all the most intimate in me, the handle in ceaseless motion that governed the rest, was my belief in philosophic richness, in the beauty of the book I was reading, and my desire to appropriate them to myself, whatever this book might be. For, even if I had bought it in Combray, it is that I had recognized it for having been mentioned to me as a remarkable work by the teacher or schoolmate who at that time seemed to me to possess the secret of truth and beauty.
Came the emotions given to me by the action in which I was taking part, for those afternoons were more full of dramatic events than often is an entire lifetime…
…joys and misfortunes of which the most intense would never be revealed to us because the slowness with which they occur clouds our perception.
Next would come, half projected before my eyes, the setting where the action was taking place…Thus was it for two summers, in the heat of the Combray garden, because of the book I was reading, that I felt nostalgic for a mountainous, river-crossed land…
DONG…
DONG
At every hour, it seemed to me it had been only a few instants since the previous one had sounded;
Sometimes even, that premature hour would ring twice more than the last;
DONG…
DONG…
DONG…
DONG
so there was one I had not heard, something that had taken place had not taken place for me;
the interest in reading, magic like a profound sleep, had fooled my hallucinating ears…
Beautiful, Sunday afternoons beneath the chestnut tree in the Combray garden, carefully emptied by me of my personal existence's mundane incidents, which I had replaced there with a life of adventures and strange aspirations within a country flowing with living waters, you still evoke that life for me whenever I think of you…
THEY'RE HERE, THEY'RE HERE!

THEY'RE HERE, THEY'RE HERE!
THEY'RE HERE!
THEY'RE HERE!
!
Those were the days when, for garrison maneuvers, the troops would cross Combray, usually taking Rue Sainte-Hildegarde.
IT'S BEAUTIFUL, ISN'T IT, MADAME FRANCOISE, TO SEE YOUNG PEOPLE WHO DON'T CARE ABOUT THEIR LIVES.
POOR CHILDREN, POOR YOUTHS WHO'LL BE MOWN DOWN LIKE A FIELD; IT'S SHOCKING JUST THINKING ABOUT IT!
DON'T CARE ABOUT THEIR LIVES? WELL, WHAT SHOULD YOU CARE ABOUT IF IT ISN'T YOUR LIFE, THE ONLY GIFT THAT THE GOOD LORD DOESN'T GIVE TWICE? GOODNESS GRACIOUS! BUT IT'S TRUE THEY DON'T CARE. I SAW 'EM IN 1870; THEY'RE NO LONGER AFRAID OF DEATH IN THOSE MISERABLE WARS; THEY'RE NOTHING MORE NOR LESS THAN MADMEN; AND THEN THEY'RE NO LONGER WORTH THE ROPE TO HANG 'EM, THEY'RE NOT MEN, THEY'RE LI-ONS!
For Françoise, there was nothing flattering being compared to a "li-on."
YOU SEE, FRANCOISE, A REVOLUTION WOULD BE BETTER, BECAUSE WHEN THEY'RE DECLARED, ONLY THOSE WHO WANT TO, GO.
OH! YES, THAT AT LEAST, IS MORE HONEST...
WHEN WAR'S DECLARED, THEY STOP ALL THE TRAINS, YOU KNOW.
OF COURSE, SO WE CAN'T FLEE!
OH! THEY'RE CUNNING...
For he would not admit that war was not some kind of bad trick that the government was trying to play on the people...

I got back to my book…
BERGOTTE
My grandfather claimed that every time I made friends with someone and brought him home, he was always a Jew…
NOW I DON'T HAVE ANYTHING AGAINST JEWS,
MY FRIEND SWANN, IN FACT, IS OF A JEWISH BACKGROUND…
IT'S JUST THAT, REALLY, YOU DON'T CHOOSE AMONG THE BEST!
So, when I'd bring home a new friend…
DI DA DA TALAM, TALIM…
I had heard tell of Bergotte for the first time from one of my friends who was older than I…Bloch.
MISTRUST YOUR RATHER CRASS PREDILECTION FOR MUSSET. HERE'S A BOOK RECOMMENDED BY MY VERY DEAR MASTER, FATHER LECONTE. HE CONSIDERS THE AUTHOR, MR. BERGOTTE ONE OF THE MOST SUBTLE FELLAS…
Naturally, he would just sing the aria "O, God of our fathers" from La Juive or "Israel, break your chains," but I was afraid my friend would recognize the tune and would figure out the words.
My grandfather's funny little habits did not imply any spiteful feelings towards my friends. But Bloch had displeased my parents for other reasons.
He had started off by irritating my father…
WHY, MONSIEUR BLOCH, WHAT'S THE WEATHER LIKE THEN? DID IT RAIN? I DON'T UNDERSTAND, THE BAROMETER CALLED FOR FAIR WEATHER.
SIR, I'M COMPLETELY INCAPABLE OF TELLING YOU IF IT'S RAINED. I LIVE SO RESOLUTELY BEYOND PHYSICAL CONTINGENCIES THAT MY SENSES DON'T TAKE THE TROUBLE OF INFORMING ME OF THEM.
Once Bloch had gone:
OH, MY POOR SON, YOUR FRIEND'S AN IDIOT. HE COULDN'T EVEN TELL ME ABOUT THE WEATHER! WHY, THERE'S NOTHING MORE INTERESTING! HE'S AN IMBECILE.
Then Bloch had displeased my grandmother.
…YES, I'M FEELING A BIT POORLY.
OH! POOR, POOR MADAME!
I CAN'T BELIEVE HE'S SINCERE, SINCE HE DOESN'T KNOW ME; OR MAYBE HE'S CRAZY.
And finally he had upset everyone because, having come to lunch an hour and a half late, covered in muck…
I NEVER ALLOW MYSELF TO BE INFLUENCED BY ATMOSPHERIC DISTURBANCES NOR BY CONVENTIONAL DIVISIONS OF TIME. I WOULD WILLINGLY REINTRODUCE THE USE OF THE OPIUM PIPE AND OF MALAYSIAN KRISS, BUT I AM IGNORANT IN THOSE INFINITELY MORE PERNICIOUS, BESIDES BEING BORINGLY MIDDLE-CLASS, INSTRUMENTS, THE WATCH AND THE UMBRELLA.
Despite all, he would have returned to Combray if, after that dinner…
…when he had just informed me that all women thought only of love and that there were not any whose resistance could not be vanquished,…
THEY SAY YOUR GREAT-AUNT HAD A STORMY YOUTH…
…MOREOVER, SHE WAS A PUBLICLY KEPT WOMAN.
I couldn't refrain from repeating these words to my parents…he was shown the door when he returned.
But he had spoken the truth concerning Bergotte.

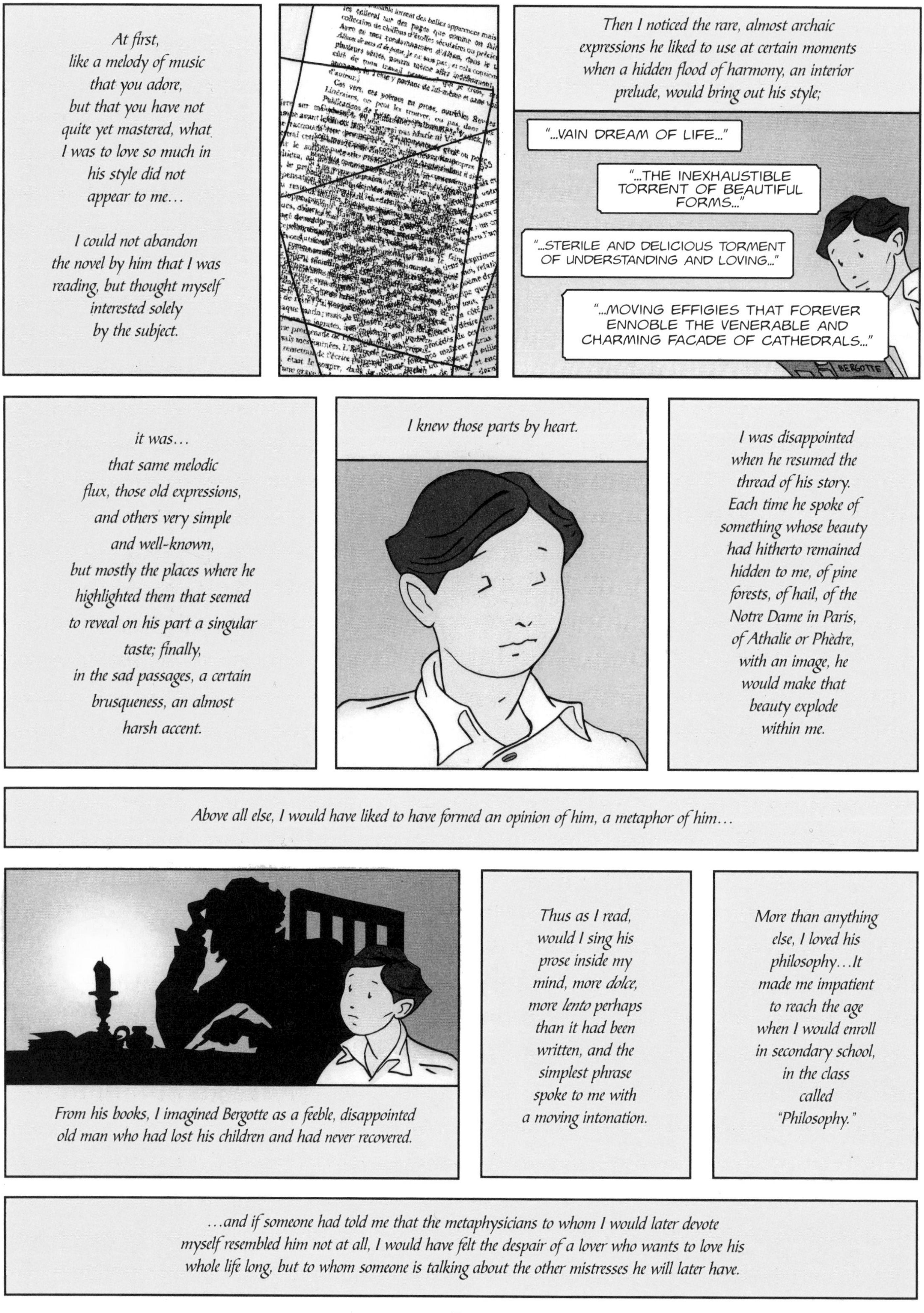
At first, like a melody of music that you adore, but that you have not quite yet mastered, what I was to love so much in his style did not appear to me…
I could not abandon the novel by him that I was reading, but thought myself interested solely by the subject.
Then I noticed the rare, almost archaic expressions he liked to use at certain moments when a hidden flood of harmony, an interior prelude, would bring out his style;
"…VAIN DREAM OF LIFE…"
"…THE INEXHAUSTIBLE TORRENT OF BEAUTIFUL FORMS…"
"…STERILE AND DELICIOUS TORMENT OF UNDERSTANDING AND LOVING…"
"…MOVING EFFIGIES THAT FOREVER ENNOBLE THE VENERABLE AND CHARMING FACADE OF CATHEDRALS…"
BERGOTTE
it was… that same melodic flux, those old expressions, and others very simple and well-known, but mostly the places where he highlighted them that seemed to reveal on his part a singular taste; finally, in the sad passages, a certain brusqueness, an almost harsh accent.
I knew those parts by heart.
I was disappointed when he resumed the thread of his story. Each time he spoke of something whose beauty had hitherto remained hidden to me, of pine forests, of hail, of the Notre Dame in Paris, of Athalie or Phèdre, with an image, he would make that beauty explode within me.
Above all else, I would have liked to have formed an opinion of him, a metaphor of him…
From his books, I imagined Bergotte as a feeble, disappointed old man who had lost his children and had never recovered.
Thus as I read, would I sing his prose inside my mind, more dolce, more lento perhaps than it had been written, and the simplest phrase spoke to me with a moving intonation.
More than anything else, I loved his philosophy…It made me impatient to reach the age when I would enroll in secondary school, in the class called "Philosophy."
…and if someone had told me that the metaphysicians to whom I would later devote myself resembled him not at all, I would have felt the despair of a lover who wants to love his whole life long, but to whom someone is talking about the other mistresses he will later have.

One Sunday…
WHAT ARE YOU READING? MAY I SEE?
WHY, IT'S BERGOTTE? WHO SUGGESTED HIS WORKS TO YOU?
MY FRIEND BLOCH DID.
AH, YES! THAT BOY I SAW HERE ONCE, WHO SO RESEMBLES BELLINI'S PORTRAIT OF MAHOMET II. IN ANY CASE, HE HAS TASTE, FOR BERGOTTE IS A CHARMING SOUL.
I KNOW HIM WELL. IF IT WOULD PLEASE YOU TO HAVE HIM INSCRIBE A FEW WORDS ON THE TITLE PAGE OF YOUR COPY, I'LL ASK HIM.
AND COULD YOU TELL ME WHICH ACTOR HE PREFERS?
I DON'T KNOW WHICH ACTOR. BUT I DO KNOW THAT HE FINDS NO MALE ACTOR THE EQUAL OF BERMA WHOM HE ESTEEMS ABOVE ALL. HAVE YOU HEARD HER?
MY PARENTS DON'T ALLOW ME TO GO TO THE THEATRE.
THAT'S UNFORTUNATE. BERMA IN PHEDRE, IN LE CID, SHE'S JUST AN ACTRESS, I SUPPOSE, BUT YOU KNOW, I DON'T VERY MUCH BELIEVE IN THE "HIERARCHY" OF THE ARTS...
When Swann used an expression that seemed to imply his opinion on an important subject, he was careful to isolate it with a special, ironic intonation, seeming not to wish to claim it for his own…
Until then, that horror of seriously expressing his opinion had seemed to me something that must be elegant and Parisian, that was opposed to provincial dogmatism…But now I found something shocking in this attitude. He seemed to not dare have an opinion…
OH, THE BALLS AT THE PRINCESSE DE LEON ARE OF NO IMPORTANCE...
Yet it was to that sort of pleasure that he devoted his life. I found it all contradictory.
For what other life would he reserve for finally saying what he thought of things, for formulating judgments he would not put between quotation marks, and for no longer devoting himself to occupations he simultaneously confessed to be ridiculous?
I CAN ALSO ASK BERGOTTE ANYTHING YOU LIKE. A WEEK DOESN'T GO BY WITHOUT HIM DINING AT MY HOUSE. HE'S MY DAUGHTER'S GOOD FRIEND. THEY GO TOGETHER TO VISIT OLD TOWNS, CATHEDRALS, AND CASTLES.
When I had learned that day that Mademoiselle Swann was a being of such a rare condition, bathing in her natural element amidst so many privileges,…
…I felt how much I would seem crude and ignorant to her, and was filled with both desire and despair .
Of all it needs to be born, what love treasures the most is for a being to participate in an unknown life where that being's love can admit us. It is why women love soldiers and firemen; they think they're kissing beneath the armor a different heart, adventurous and sweet.

While I was reading in the garden…
...AND I JUST SAW MME. GOUPIL GOING BY WITHOUT AN UMBRELLA, WITH THE SILK DRESS THAT SHE HAD MADE AT CHATEAUDUN. IF SHE HAS VERY FAR TO GO BEFORE VESPERS, SHE COULD GET IT SOAKED.
MAYBE, MAYBE...
WHY, THAT REMINDS ME THAT I NEVER LEARNED IF SHE MADE IT TO CHURCH BEFORE THE ELEVATION. I'LL HAVE TO REMEMBER TO ASK EULALIE...
FRANCOISE, JUST YOU LOOK AT THAT BLACK CLOUD BEHIND THE STEEPLE AND THAT POOR LIGHT ON THE SLATES, SURELY THE DAY WON'T GO BY WITHOUT ANY RAIN.
IT COULDN'T GO ON SO, IT WAS TOO HOT.
AND THE SOONER THE BETTER, BECAUSE AS LONG AS THE STORM HASN'T BROKEN, MY VICHY WATER WON'T GO DOWN.
MAYBE, MAYBE...
WHAT, THREE O'CLOCK? BUT VESPERS HAVE GOTTEN STARTED AND I'VE FORGOTTEN MY PEPSIN!
NOW I UNDERSTAND WHY MY VICHY WATER HAS BEEN ON MY STOMACH.
THREE O'CLOCK, IT'S INCREDIBLE HOW TIME FLIES!
TOC
TOC
TOC
TOC
SEE? WHAT WAS I SAYING, FRANCOISE?
GLIING

FRANCOISE, RUN ALONG AND SEE WHO COULD BE OUT IN SUCH WEATHER.
Françoise returned:
IT'S MME. AMADEE WHO SAID SHE WAS GOING FOR A WALK. BUT IT'S RAINING HARD!
THAT DOESN'T SURPRISE ME AT ALL. I'VE ALWAYS SAID HER MIND DOESN'T WORK LIKE OTHER PEOPLE'S.
MME. AMADEE'S ALWAYS THE OPPOSITE OF EVERYONE ELSE.
Françoise would reserve the moment when she was alone with the other servants for saying that she thought my grandmother a bit "loony."
THE BENEDICTION'S OVER NOW! EULALIE WON'T BE COMING NOW; THE WEATHER WILL HAVE GIVEN HER A SCARE.
BUT IT'S ONLY FOUR-THIRTY, MADAME OCTAVE.
AH, EULALIE!
HELLO, MME. OCTAVE.
I'LL LEAVE YOU, MADAME OCTAVE.
Unfortunately, scarcely had Eulalie been admitted when…
THE PRIEST WOULD BE CHARMED, DELIGHTED, IF MME. OCTAVE ISN'T RESTING, IF SHE COULD RECEIVE HIM.
THE PRIEST DOESN'T WANT TO BE A BOTHER. HE IS DOWNSTAIRS, I TOLD HIM TO GO INTO THE PARLOR.
In reality, the priest's visits were not as great a pleasure to my aunt as Françoise supposed… The priest, accustomed to giving information to distinguished visitors about the church, would tire her with infinite explanations and, moreover, always the same ones.
But when it occurred right at the same time as Eulalie's, his visit frankly became unpleasant for my aunt. She would have preferred to make the most of Eulalie and not have everyone at the same time…
But she did not dare to not receive him…
MY DEAR PRIEST, THEY'VE BEEN TELLING ME AN ARTIST HAS SET UP HIS EASEL IN YOUR CHURCH TO COPY A WINDOW...
...THE UGLIEST ONE IN THE CHURCH...

I WOULDN'T GO SO FAR AS TO SAY IT'S THE UGLIEST ONE, BECAUSE IF THERE ARE PARTS OF SAINT-HILAIRE THAT DESERVE TO BE VISITED, THERE ARE SOME OTHERS THAT ARE RATHER OLD IN MY POOR BASILICA, THE ONLY ONE IN ALL THE DIOCESE THAT HASN'T BEEN RESTORED.
MY LORD, THE ENTRANCE IS DIRTY AND ANTIQUATED, BUT AT LEAST OF A MAJESTIC CHARACTER; THE SAME GOES FOR THE TAPESTRIES OF ESTHER, WHICH I PERSONALLY WOULDN'T GIVE TWO CENTS FOR, BUT WHICH ARE RANKED SECOND ONLY TO THOSE OF SENS BY THE CONNOISSEURS.
BUT DON'T GET ME STARTED ABOUT THE WINDOWS!
DOES IT MAKE GOOD SENSE TO HAVE WINDOWS THAT DON'T LET IN ANY LIGHT AND EVEN CONFUSE YOUR SIGHT, IN A CHURCH WHERE NO TWO SLABS ARE ON THE SAME LEVEL, WHICH THEY REFUSE TO REPLACE FOR ME ON THE PRETEXT THAT THEY'RE THE TOMBS OF THE ABBOTS OF COMBRAY AND THE LORDS OF GUERMANTES?
INRI
I'M SURE THAT IF YOU ASKED THE MONSIGNOR HE'D NOT REFUSE YOU A NEW STAINED-GLASS WINDOW...
BUT IT'S THE MONSIGNOR HIMSELF WHO STARTED THE FUSS ABOUT THAT BLASTED WINDOW BY PROVING THAT IT'S A PICTURE OF GILBERT THE BAD, A LORD OF GUERMANTES, THE DIRECT DESCENDANT OF GENEVIEVE DE BRABANT, THE MAIDEN OF GUERMANTES, RECEIVING ABSOLUTION FROM SAINT HILAIRE!
BUT I DON'T SEE WHERE SAINT HILAIRE IS?
SURE, IN THE CORNER OF THE WINDOW, YOU NEVER NOTICED THE WOMAN IN YELLOW? WELL! IT'S SAINT HILAIRE WHO'S ALSO CALLED SAINT ILLIERS, SAINT HELIER AND EVEN SAINT YLIE. THESE VARIOUS CORRUPTIONS OF "SANCTUS HILARIUS" AREN'T, MOREOVER, THE MOST CURIOUS. THUS YOUR PATRON SAINT, MY DEAR EULALIE, YOU KNOW WHAT BECAME OF HER? SAINT ELOI: SHE BECAME A MALE SAINT. DO YOU SEE, EULALIE, AFTER YOU'RE DEAD, THEY'LL MAKE A MAN OF YOU?...
MY DEAR PRIEST, YOU'RE ALWAYS MAKING FUN!
BUT WHAT IS INCONTESTABLY THE MOST CURIOUS IN OUR CHURCH IS THE GRANDIOSE PERSPECTIVE THAT YOU HAVE FROM THE STEEPLE. I WOULDN'T ADVISE YOU TO CLIMB OUR NINETY-SEVEN STEPS, ALL THE MORE SINCE YOU CLIMB DOUBLED OVER IF YOU DON'T WANT TO CRACK YOUR HEAD. IN ANY EVENT, YOU HAVE TO COVER UP WELL, BECAUSE THERE'S QUITE A DRAFT ONCE YOU GET UP THERE!
NONETHELESS, ON SUNDAYS THERE ARE ALWAYS GROUPS COMING EVEN FROM FAR AWAY TO ADMIRE THE BEAUTY OF THE PANORAMA...

WHEN THE SKY'S CLEAR, YOU CAN SEE ALL THE WAY TO VERNEUIL. ESPECIALLY, YOU CAN TAKE IN THINGS AT THE SAME TIME THAT YOU CAN'T USUALLY SEE FROM ONE OR THE OTHER, LIKE THE COURSE OF THE VIVONNE AND THE DITCHES OF SAINT-ASSISE-LES-COMBRAY WHICH ARE SEPARATED BY A VEIL OF TALL TREES, OR ALSO THE DIFFERENT CANALS OF JOUY-LE-VICOMTE.
EVERY TIME I'VE GONE TO JOUY-LE-VICOMTE, I'VE SEEN ONE END OF THE CANAL WELL ENOUGH, THEN, WHEN I HAD TURNED INTO A STREET, I'D SEE ANOTHER, BUT THEN I'D NO LONGER SEE THE PREVIOUS ONE. I MIGHT WELL PUT THEM TOGETHER IN MY MIND, BUT IT WASN'T VERY EFFECTIVE.
FROM THE STEEPLE OF SAINT-HILAIRE, IT'S SOMETHING ELSE ALTOGETHER, THE AREA'S CAUGHT UP IN A ENTIRE NETWORK. EXCEPT YOU CAN'T SEE ANY WATER; YOU'D SAY THERE WERE GREAT CRACKS CUTTING THE TOWN INTO QUARTERS, JUST AS IF IT WERE A BRIOCHE WHOSE PIECES WERE HOLDING TOGETHER, BUT WHICH ARE ALREADY SLICED.

The priest had so fatigued my aunt that, scarcely had he departed, she was obliged to send away Eulalie.

HERE, MY POOR EULALIE, THIS IS SO YOU WON'T FORGET ME IN YOUR PRAYERS.

AH! BUT, MADAME OCTAVE, I DON'T KNOW IF I SHOULD, YOU KNOW I DON'T COME FOR THAT!

…Eulalie would say with the same hesitation and the same embarassment, every time, as if it were the first, and with an appearance of discontent, which cheered my aunt and did not displease her, for if Eulalie one day, while taking the coin, seemed less bothered than usual, my aunt would say:

I DON'T KNOW WHAT'S WRONG WITH EULALIE. THOUGH I GAVE HER THE SAME AMOUNT AS ALWAYS, SHE DIDN'T SEEM VERY HAPPY.

I THINK SHE DOESN'T HAVE MUCH TO COMPLAIN ABOUT!
It wasn't that Françoise wanted the money my aunt gave to Eulalie for herself. She enjoyed all that my aunt possessed sufficiently, aware that the mistress' wealth simultaneously embellished her servant in the eyes of all…
She was stingy only for my aunt's sake;
However, she would not have found any harm in my aunt allowing herself to give, if only it had been to the rich…
Perhaps she thought that they, having no need of my aunt's gifts, could not be suspected of loving her because of them.
FLATTERERS KNOW HOW TO GET THEMSELVES IN GOOD GRACES FOR PROFIT. BUT BE PATIENT, THE GOOD LORD WILL PUNISH THEM ALL ONE FINE DAY!
MADAME OCTAVE, I'LL LET YOU GET SOME REST, YOU SEEM VERY TIRED.
VICHY
BOOM
BOOM
BOOM
BOOM
HAS EULALIE ALREADY LEFT? DO YOU KNOW I FORGOT TO ASK HER IF MME. GOUPIL ARRIVED AT MASS BEFORE THE ELEVATION! QUICK, RUN AFTER HER!
But Françoise came back,
not having been able to catch Eulalie.
IT'S ANNOYING. IT WAS THE ONLY IMPORTANT THING I HAD TO ASK HER.
Thus did life go by for my aunt Léonie, ever the same, in the calm uniformity of what she called her "little routine." It was preserved by everyone…even in the village where, three streets from us, a worker, before nailing up his crates, would have Françoise asked if my aunt "weren't resting."

On Saturdays, during the month of May, we would leave after dinner to go to the "Month of Mary."
LET'S SEE THAT NOTHING'S WRONG WITH YOUR CLOTHES: MR. VINTEUIL WILL SURELY BE THERE AND HE'S VERY SEVERE ABOUT WHAT HE CALLS "THE DEPLORABLE STYLE OF UNTIDY YOUNGSTERS, IN KEEPING WITH PRESENT TIMES."
It was in the month of Mary that I recall having begun to love hawthorns...inseparable from the mysteries of the celebration in which they took part, ...festively prepared, made pretty by the festoons of their foliage upon which was profusely strewn, as on a bridal train, small buds of a striking whiteness.
But without daring to look at them except surreptiously, I felt that these pompous foundations were alive and that nature herself, by hollowing out those indentations in the leaves, by adding the supreme ornament of these white buttons, had made this decoration worthy of what was both a public rejoicing and a mystic solemnity.
Mr. Vinteuil had come with his daughter to sit beside us.
From a good family, he had been my grandmother's sisters' piano teacher and when, after the death of his wife and coming into an inheritance, he had retired near Combray, he was often invited to our house. But, of an excessive prudishness, he ceased coming in order to not encounter Swann who had contracted what he called "an unsuitable marriage, in fashion nowadays."

My mother, having learned that he composed, had told him out of kindness that when she came to see him, he would have to let her hear something by him. M. Vinteuil would have had much pleasure in doing so, but he held to politeness and kindness so scrupulously that, always putting himself in the place of others, he was afraid of bothering them and seeming egotistical to them if he followed his desires or simply let them be guessed.
The day my parents had gone to visit him, I had accompanied them...
MAY I STAY OUTSIDE AND PLAY?
YES, GO AHEAD, IF YOU WANT, BUT DON'T WANDER TOO FAR.
Since Montjouvain, Mr. Vinteuil's house, lay below a shrubby mound where I had hidden, I found myself on the same level as his parlor...
When he was told of my parents' visit, I saw M. Vinteuil hasten to lay a piece of music in the open on the piano.
But, once my parents had come in, he grabbed it and put it in a corner.
I BEG YOU, PLAY THAT PIECE.
WHY, I DON'T KNOW WHO LEFT THAT ON THE PIANO, IT DOESN'T BELONG THERE!
His sole passion was for his daughter, and she, who looked like a boy, seemed so robust that you could barely keep from smiling seeing the precautions her father would take for her...
At the moment of leaving the church, I smelled a bittersweet scent of almonds escaping from the hawthorn...
I WAS VERY HAPPY TO SEE YOU.
COME, MY DEAR, YOU SHOULD COVER UP.
And they both returned to Montjouvain.

One Sunday, when my aunt had had a simultaneous visit from the priest and Eulalie and had then rested, we all went up to say goodnight, and mama was consoling her on the bad luck that always brought her visitors at the same time:
I KNOW THAT THINGS WORKED OUT BADLY AGAIN THIS AFTERNOON, LEONIE, YOU HAD ALL YOUR COMPANY AT ONCE.
AN ABUNDANCE OF WEALTH...
I WANT TO TAKE ADVANTAGE OF THE WHOLE FAMILY BEING TOGETHER...I'M AFRAID THAT WE'VE GOTTEN ON BAD TERMS WITH M. LEGRANDIN: HE BARELY SAID HELLO TO ME THIS MORNING...
...When M. Legrandin had passed near us while exiting the church, walking beside a lady of the neighborhood that we only knew by sight, my father had greeted him in both a friendly and reserved manner...
?!
...I'D BE ALL THE MORE SORRY THINKING HIM ANGRY, THERE AMONG ALL THOSE FOLKS IN THEIR SUNDAY BEST... HE SEEMS SO UNAFFECTED...AND HAS AN ALMOST INGENUOUS AIR THAT IS ALTOGETHER LIKEABLE.
But the family council was unanimously of the opinion that my father had imagined it, or that Legrandin, at that moment, was absorbed in some thought.
Besides, my father's fears vanished the next evening. While we were returning from a long walk...
AH, IT'S M. LEGRANDIN!
DO YOU KNOW, MISTER BOOKWORM, THIS VERSE BY PAUL DESJARDINS: "THE WOODS ARE ALREADY DARK, THE SKY IS STILL BLUE." ISN'T THAT A FINE NOTE ON THIS VERY HOUR?
MAY THE SKIES ALWAYS BE BLUE FOR YOU, MY YOUNG FRIEND; AND EVEN IN THE HOUR, WHICH IS COMING FOR ME, WHEN THE WOODS ARE ALREADY DARK, YOU WILL CONSOLE YOURSELF BY LOOKING TOWARDS THE SKY.
FAREWELL, MY FRIENDS!

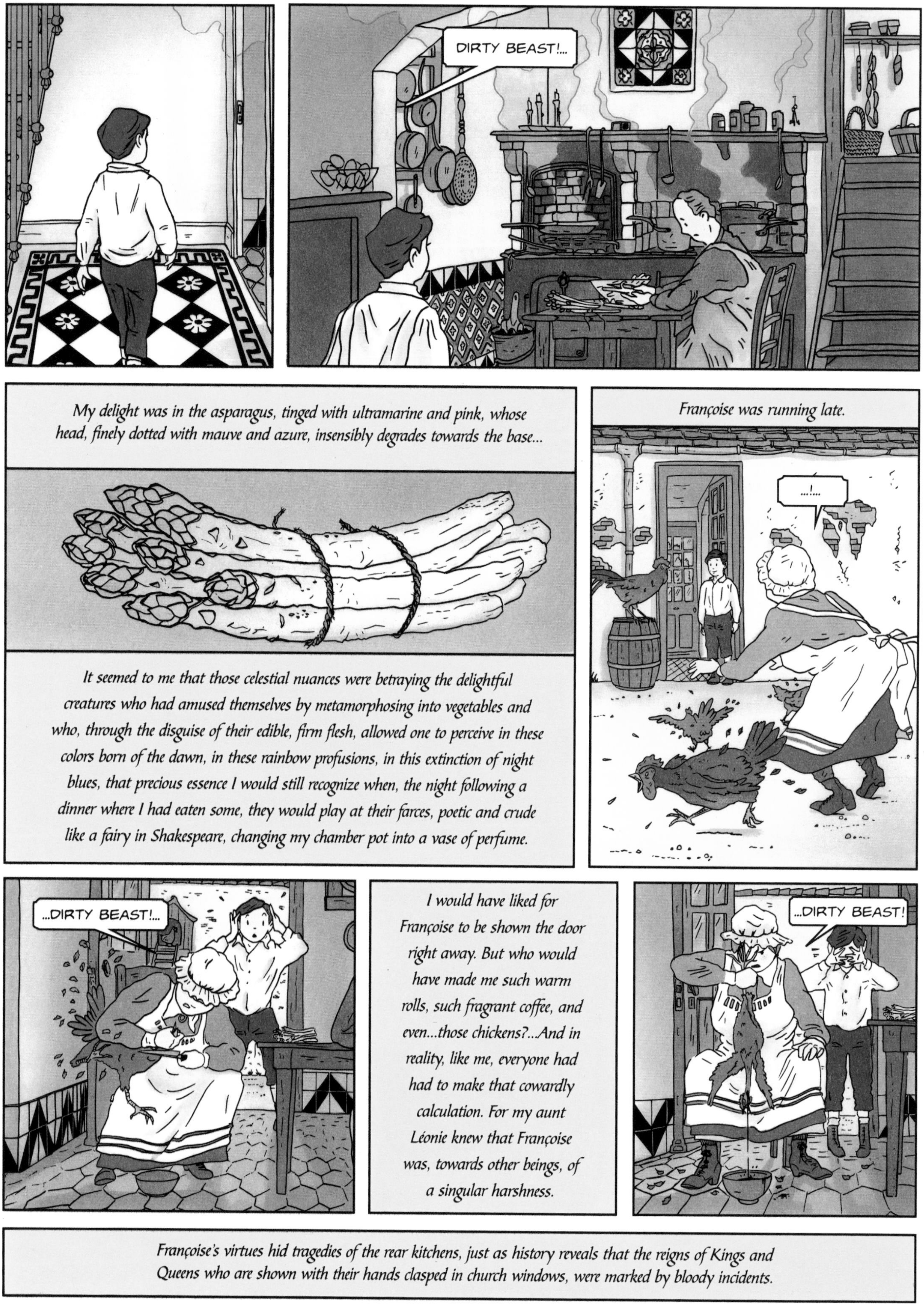

DIRTY BEAST!...
My delight was in the asparagus, tinged with ultramarine and pink, whose head, finely dotted with mauve and azure, insensibly degrades towards the base...
It seemed to me that those celestial nuances were betraying the delightful creatures who had amused themselves by metamorphosing into vegetables and who, through the disguise of their edible, firm flesh, allowed one to perceive in these colors born of the dawn, in these rainbow profusions, in this extinction of night blues, that precious essence I would still recognize when, the night following a dinner where I had eaten some, they would play at their farces, poetic and crude like a fairy in Shakespeare, changing my chamber pot into a vase of perfume.
Françoise was running late.
...!...
...DIRTY BEAST!...
I would have liked for Françoise to be shown the door right away. But who would have made me such warm rolls, such fragrant coffee, and even...those chickens?...And in reality, like me, everyone had had to make that cowardly calculation. For my aunt Léonie knew that Françoise was, towards other beings, of a singular harshness.
...DIRTY BEAST!
Françoise's virtues hid tragedies of the rear kitchens, just as history reveals that the reigns of Kings and Queens who are shown with their hands clasped in church windows, were marked by bloody incidents.

The torrents of tears she would shed while reading the newspaper about the misfortunes of someone unknown would quickly dry up if she could imagine in a more precise manner the person whom it concerned.
One of those nights following the kitchen-girl's delivery, the latter was seized with horrible pains: mama heard her moaning, got up, and awoke Françoise.
WHY, MADAME! SHE'S JUST PRETENDING, SHE'S ACTING LIKE SHE'S THE MISTRESS...
The doctor, who had feared these attacks:
I LEFT A MARKER IN YOUR MEDICINE BOOK, FOR THE FIRST AID TO GIVE...
FRANCOISE, GO LOOK FOR THE BOOK IN THE LIBRARY, AND ABOVE ALL, DON'T LET THE MARKER DROP OUT!
An hour later, Françoise had not yet returned;
OHHOHO...OH HO HO...
MY GOD MY GOD!
ALAS, BLESSED VIRGIN, IS IT POSSIBLE THAT THE GOOD LORD WOULD ALLOW AN UNFORTUNATE HUMAN CREATURE TO SUFFER SO? OH, THE POOR THING!
but no sooner had I called her and she had returned near the bed of Giotto's Charity, her tears instantly ceased to flow; and, at the sight of the same suffering whose description had made her cry, she now produced only the grumblings of ill humor, even dreadful sarcasm...
SHE OUGHT NOT TO HAVE DONE WHAT CAUSES THAT! SHE'D BETTER NOT TAKE ON AIRS NOW!
ALL THE SAME, THE BOY WOULD'VE HAD TO HAVE BEEN ABANDONED BY THE GOOD LORD TO GO WITH "THAT." AH! IT'S JUST LIKE THEY USED TO SAY IN MY POOR MOTHER'S PATOIS:
"IF YOU FALL FOR A BITCH'S ASS, IT'LL SMELL LIKE A ROSE."
Many years later, we learned that that summer we had eaten asparagus almost every day because their odor gave the poor kitchen-girl responsible for cleaning them asthma attacks of such severity that she was obliged in the end to leave our service.

I dined with Legrandin on his terrace. Just the day before, he had asked my parents to send me to dine that evening with him. They wondered at the house whether they ought to send me, all the same, to dine with M. Legrandin.
COME KEEP YOUR OLD FRIEND COMPANY,...
...COME WITH THE GLORIOUS, SILK RAIMENT OF LILIES WORTHY OF SOLOMON, AND THE POLYCHROME ENAMEL OF THOUGHTS, BUT COME ESPECIALLY WITH THE BREEZE STILL FRESH WITH THE LAST FROSTS AND WHICH WILL TEASE OPEN, FOR THE TWO BUTTERFLIES WHO'VE BEEN WAITING AT THE DOOR SINCE THIS MORNING, THE FIRST ROSE OF JERUSALEM.
...But my grandmother refused to believe that he had been impolite.
THERE'S A PRETTY QUALITY TO SILENCE, ISN'T THERE?...IT COMES INTO LIFE ONE HOUR...WHERE THE ONLY MUSIC EARS CAN HEAR ANY LONGER IS THAT WHICH THE MOONBEAM PLAYS ON THE FLUTE OF SILENCE.
DO YOU KNOW, SIR, THE LADY... THE LADIES OF GUERMANTES?
!
The ring of his eyelid darkened, lowered. And his mouth, marked by a bitter line, getting a hold of itself more quickly, smiled, whereas his look remained pained, like that of a beautiful martyr whose body's prickling with arrows:
...NO,...I DON'T KNOW THEM.
...NO,...NO, I DON'T KNOW THEM, I NEVER WANTED TO; DEEP DOWN, I HAVE A JACOBIN MIND.
DEEP DOWN, IN THE WORLD, I ONLY STILL LOVE SOME CHURCHES, TWO OR THREE BOOKS, SCARCELY A FEW MORE PAINTINGS, AND THE MOONLIGHT WHEN THE BREEZE OF YOUR YOUTH REACHES ME...
But, what I understood was that Legrandin was not being entirely truthful when he said he only loved the churches, the moonlight, and youth;
He very much loved the people in castles...He was a snob.
And if I asked:
DO YOU KNOW THE GUERMANTES?
Legrandin...in a moment pierced and stricken like a Saint Sebastian of snobbery:
ALAS! HOW YOU HAVE HURT ME! NO, I DON'T KNOW THE GUERMANTES, DON'T REAWAKEN THE GREATEST SORROW OF MY LIFE.

There were around Combray, two "ways" for walking, and in such opposite directions that we would not, in fact, go out by the same door when we wanted to go one way or the other: the Méséglise-la-Vineuse way, that people also called "Swann's way" because you passed in front of Mr. Swann's property to get there, and the Guermantes' way.
THE MESEGLISE WAY? THE PRETTIEST VIEW OF THE PLAIN I KNOW OF!
THE GUERMANTES' WAY? TYPICAL OF A LANDSCAPE OF RIVERS.
So, "going the Guermantes' way" to get to Méséglise, or the contrary, seemed to me an expression devoid of sense, like heading east in order to go west.
One day:
DO YOU REMEMBER SWANN SAYING YESTERDAY THAT, SINCE HIS WIFE AND DAUGHTER WERE LEAVING FOR REIMS, HE WOULD TAKE ADVANTAGE AND GO SPEND A DAY IN PARIS? WE COULD WALK ALONG THE PARK, SINCE THE LADIES AREN'T THERE, IT WOULD SHORTEN IT FOR US ACCORDINGLY.
CERTAINLY, WE'LL SPARE OURSELVES A GOOD DETOUR!
...AND THAT POND WAS PUT IN BY SWANN'S PARENTS...
The departure of Mlle. Swann...made the contemplation of Tansonville indifferent to me the first time it was permitted me...
I would have liked for a miracle to have made Mlle. Swann appear with her father, so close to us that we would not have had the time to avoid them and would have been obliged to make her acquaintance.
...HASN'T CHANGED SINCE THE DEATH OF SWANN'S MOTHER, THESE TREES, ON THE OTHER HAND...
?
Thus, when suddenly I saw on the lawn, like a sign of her possible presence...
!
WELL, ARE YOU COMING?

When I had to run to catch up with my father and grandfather on the little path climbing towards the fields,...
...I found it all abuzz with the smell of hawthorns.
!
YOU WHO LOVE HAWTHORNS, COME LOOK AT THIS PINK ONE; IT'S PRETTY!
It was in fact a hawthorn, but pink, even prettier than the white ones. ... "In color," and therefore of a superior quality, according to the price scale in the "store" in the square or at Camus' where those cookies that were pink were more expensive. For my part, I had a higher opinion of cream cheese that was pink, the one in which I had been allowed to crush some strawberries.
?!
A young girl...was watching us, looking up, her face strewn with pink stains.
Her black eyes were shining and, ...for long, each time I thought of her again, the memory of their radiance would immediately appear to me like that of a bright azure, since she was blond.

She allowed her gaze to drift my way without seeming to see me, but with an intensity and concealed smile that I could interpret only as proof of offensive scorn.
...and her hand sketched an indecent gesture at the same time...
COME ALONG, GILBERTE!
WHAT ARE YOU DOING?
THAT POOR SWANN, WHAT A GAME THEY'RE MAKING HIM PLAY: THEY GET HIM TO LEAVE SO SHE CAN STAY HERE ALONE WITH HER CHARLUS, BECAUSE IT'S HIM, I RECOGNIZED HIM! AND THE LITTLE GIRL, MIXED UP IN THAT INFAMY.
Gilberte...I was in love with her, I was sorry to not have had the time or inspiration to offend her, to hurt her, and to force her to remember me. I found her so beautiful...And already the charm with which her name had perfumed this place beneath the pink hawthorns was going to win over, to coat, to embalm everything that came near it...

That year, on the morning of our departure, although I had had my hair curled for a photograph and had had a hat carefully place on my head, my mother found me in tears in the small steep area adjacent to Tansonville, saying a long farewell to the hawthorns, encircling prickly branches with my arms.

AH! THERE HE IS.

OH, MY POOR LITTLE HAWTHORNS, YOU WOULDN'T FORCE ME TO LEAVE YOU! I'LL LOVE YOU FOREVER...

And, wiping away my tears, I promised them, when I was grown, to not imitate the foolish life of other men and, even in Paris, on spring days, instead of going to pay visits or to listen to rubbish, to go to the country to see the first hawthorn blooms.

The wind was always with you on the Méséglise way....I knew that Mlle. Swann often went to Laon... and when, on hot afternoons, I would see a gust, coming from the far horizon, bowing the wheat,...spreading like waves, ...this plain that was common to both of us seemed to make us closer, to unite us, I would think that the same gust had passed near her, that it was a message that she was whispering to me...and that I was kissing her in passing.

It was on the Méséglise way, at Montjouvain, that Mr. Vinteuil resided. Thus did we often cross his daughter on the road, driving a buggy at top speed.

Starting in a certain year, we no longer ran into her alone, but with an older friend, a girl with a bad reputation in the area who one day moved to Montjouvain for good.

OH WELL! IT SEEMS THAT SHE MAKES MUSIC WITH HER FRIEND, MLLE. VINTEUIL. THAT SEEMS TO SURPRISE YOU. I DON'T KNOW MYSELF. IT'S OLD VINTEUIL WHO TOLD ME HIMSELF JUST YESTERDAY. AFTER ALL, SHE HAS EVERY RIGHT TO LIKE MUSIC, THAT GAL DOES.

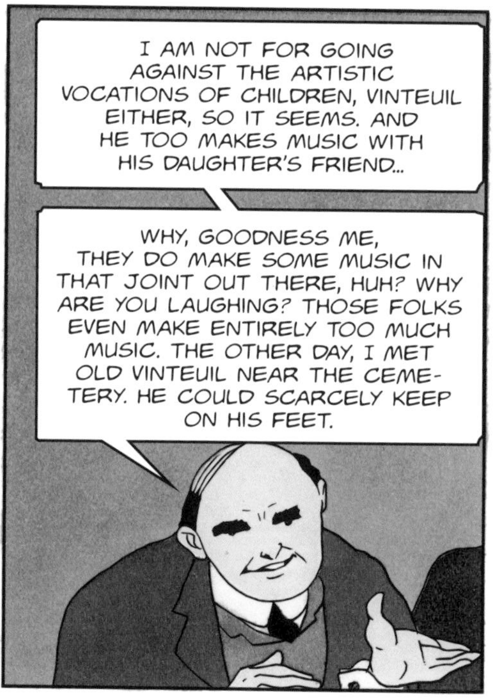
I AM NOT FOR GOING AGAINST THE ARTISTIC VOCATIONS OF CHILDREN, VINTEUIL EITHER, SO IT SEEMS. AND HE TOO MAKES MUSIC WITH HIS DAUGHTER'S FRIEND...
WHY, GOODNESS ME, THEY DO MAKE SOME MUSIC IN THAT JOINT OUT THERE, HUH? WHY ARE YOU LAUGHING? THOSE FOLKS EVEN MAKE ENTIRELY TOO MUCH MUSIC. THE OTHER DAY, I MET OLD VINTEUIL NEAR THE CEMETERY. HE COULD SCARCELY KEEP ON HIS FEET.

For those at the time who saw Mr. Vinteuil avoiding the people he knew, aging in a few months, becoming absorbed in his chagrin, spending whole days at the tomb of his wife, it would have been difficult not to understand that he was in the process of dying from grief.
But, even if Mr. Vinteuil was perhaps aware of his daughter's conduct, it did not follow that his worship of her had been diminished.
But when Mr. Vinteuil considered his daughter and himself from the perspective of their reputation, he saw himself with his daughter at their very lowest...
One day when we were walking with Swann in a Combray street...
OH! UH, HELLO.
!
And Swann, with that arrogant charity of a man of the world who, amid the dissolution of all his moral prejudices, finds in another's infamy simply a reason for acting toward him with benevolence, the tokens of which titillate the self-respect of the one giving them all the more when he feels them to be more precious to the one receiving them, spoke at length with Mr. Vinteuil, to whom he had never spoken a word till then...
...AND WHY DON'T YOU SEND YOUR DAUGHTER TO PLAY ONE DAY AT TANSONVILLE? MY DAUGHTER GILBERTE WOULD BE DELIGHTED.
It was an invitation that would have made Mr. Vinteuil indignant two years before, but that now filled him with such grateful feelings that he thought himself obliged by them to not have the indiscretion of accepting it.
Once Swann had left us...
WHAT A CHARMING MAN! WHAT A CHARMING MAN! HOW UNFORTUNATE THAT HE GOT INTO SUCH AN UNSUITABLE MARRIAGE!
And so...my parents, along with Mr. Vinteuil, deplored Swann's marriage in the name of principles and proprieties, which they seemed to suggest had not been contravened at Montjouvain.
Mr. Vinteuil did not send his daughter to Swann's. And the latter was the first one to regret it. For, every time he had just parted from Mr. Vinteuil, he recalled that for some time he had some information to ask him concerning someone who shared the same name as he, one of his relatives, Swann thought...

We had to come to Combray for the settling of my aunt Léonie's estate, for she had finally died, leaving triumphant simultaneously those who claimed that her debilitating way of life would end up killing her, and no less the others who had always maintained that she was suffering not from an imaginary, but organic, ailment, the evidence of which skeptics would be quite obliged to admit once she had succumbed to it.
FRANCOISE DIDN'T LEAVE MME. OCTAVE FOR AN INSTANT. SHE WOULDN'T UNDRESS, ALLOWED NO ONE ELSE TO CARE FOR HER. SHE DIDN'T LEAVE YOUR AUNT'S BODY UNTIL IT WAS BURIED!
That autumn, entirely occupied with the formalities to complete, meetings with lawyers and farmers, my parents got into the habit of letting me walk without them on the Méséglise way...
THAT IS NO WAY TO DRESS FOR SUCH AN OCCASION...
YOU KNOW, FRANCOISE, IF I MISS MY AUNT, IT'S BECAUSE SHE WAS A GOOD WOMAN, DESPITE HER ABSURDITIES, BUT NOT AT ALL BECAUSE SHE WAS MY AUNT. SHE COULD HAVE BEEN MY AUNT AND SEEMED ODIOUS TO ME, HER DEATH NOT CAUSING ME ANY GRIEF AT ALL.
OH!
YOU KNOW VERY WELL THAT I DON'T KNOW HOW TO ANSWER SINCE I CAN'T EXPRESS MYSELF...
ALL THE SAME, SHE WAS ONE OF YOUR "RELATIONSHIPS"...
THERE'S ALWAYS THE RESPECT YOU OWE TO YOUR "RELATIONSHIPS"...
IT'S GOOD OF ME TO CHAT WITH AN ILLITERATE WHO MAKES SUCH MALAPROPISMS!

It is perhaps from an impression gained near Montjouvain,...
...an impression remaining obscure at the time, from which came, much later, the idea that I got about sadism.
The weather was very hot; having gone all the way to the pond at Montjouvain...I had lain down in the shade and fallen asleep...
I saw before me Mlle. Vinteuil, who had probably just returned...
...in that room where her father had welcomed mine and which she had made into a small parlor of her own.
I saw all of her movements without her seeing me, but by leaving, I would have made some noise in the bushes, she would have heard me and might have believed that I had hidden there to spy on her.
She was in deep mourning for her father who had recently died.
At that moment when the rolling wheels of a carriage arriving from the road rang out...

LEAVE THEM ALL OPEN, I'M HOT.
BUT HOW ANNOYING, SOMEONE WILL SEE US!
WHEN I SAY "SEE US," I MEAN THEY'LL SEE US READING; IT'S ANNOYING, WHENEVER YOU'RE DOING SOMETHING INSIGNIFICANT, THINKING THAT THERE ARE EYES WATCHING YOU...
YES, IT'S LIKELY THAT WE'RE BEING WATCHED AT THIS HOUR, IN THIS BUSY COUNTRYSIDE!
AND SO WHAT? EVEN IF THEY COULD SEE US, IT'D BE BETTER IF THEY DO.
MADEMOISELLE SEEMS TO ME TO BE HAVING RATHER LEWD THOUGHTS THIS EVENING!

OH!...
...THAT PORTRAIT OF MY FATHER WATCHING US, I DON'T KNOW WHO COULD HAVE PUT IT THERE, YET I'VE SAID OVER AND OVER THAT IT DOESN'T BELONG THERE.
I remembered that those were the words Mr. Vinteuil had spoken to my father concerning the piece of music. That portrait no doubt regularly served in ritual profanations, for her friend answered with these words that must have been part of her liturgical responses:
OH, LEAVE HIM WHERE HE IS, HE'S NOT AROUND TO ANNOY US ANYMORE. DO YOU THINK HE'D START WHINING, THAT HE'D WANT TO PUT ON YOUR JACKET, IF HE SAW YOU THERE, WITH THE WINDOW OPEN, THAT UGLY MONKEY.
OH, NOW, NOW...
YOU KNOW WHAT I WANT TO DO TO THAT OLD HORROR?
... ...
OH! YOU WOULDN'T DARE.
" I WOULDN'T DARE SPIT ON IT? ON "THAT"?
I could hear no more.
I now knew what, for all the suffering that Mr. Vinteuil had endured during his life because of his daughter,...
he had gotten in reward after his death.
Sadists of the sort of Mlle. Vinteuil are beings so purely sentimental, so naturally virtuous, that even sensual pleasure seems something bad to them, the privilege of the wicked. And when they permit themselves to indulge for a moment, they try to impersonate the wicked and have their accomplice do so, so as to have had for a moment the illusion of having escaped from their scrupulous and tender souls into the inhuman world of pleasure.

If it was easy to go the Méséglise way, it was another matter to go the Guermantes' way, for it was a long walk and you had better be sure of what the weather would be like.
TOMORROW, IF THE WEATHER HOLDS, WE'LL GO THE GUERMANTES' WAY.
The greatest charm of the Guermantes' way was that you almost always had the course of the Vivonne along side you.
The Old Bridge led to a towing path that, at that place, was covered with the bluish foliage of hazel under which a fisherman had taken root.
PAPA, THAT GENTLE-MAN, WHAT'S HIS...
SHHH!...THE FISH!
...In Combray, that fisherman was the only person whose identity I never discovered.
On the other side, the bank was low, stretching out into vast fields all the way to the village.
They were strewn with the remains, half-buried in the grass, of the castle of the old counts of Combray who, in the Middle Ages, had the Vivonne on this side as a defense against the lords of Guermantes.

I enjoyed watching the kids putting carafes in the Vivonne to capture little minnows.
I promised myself to come there later with some lines.
MAMA, PLEASE GIVE ME A LITTLE BREAD FROM OUR SNACK TO MAKE SOME BREAD BALLS!
PLOC
PLOC
Soon the course of the Vivonne was choked with water plants...such as the water-lily endlessly going back and forth...
...making one think of certain victims of depression, amongst whose number my grandfather counted my aunt Léonie.

DONG
DONG
Sometimes, we would come up on a so-called "week-end" house, isolated, lost, ...
...a young woman who no doubt had come, according to folklore, "to bury herself there"...
...One felt that, in her renunciation, she had voluntarily left the places where she could at least have seen the one she loved, for those places which had never seen him.
Never, during the walks on the Guermantes' way, were we able to reach the sources of the Vivonne...
Neither were we ever able to go as far as I had so wished to reach, all the way to Guermantes.

I knew that the lord and lady resided there, the duke and duchess of Guermantes, I knew that they were flesh-and-blood people, but every time I thought of them, I imagined them...
...sometimes in a tapestry, as was the countess of Guermantes, in the "Crowning of Esther" in our church, ...
...sometimes in shifting colors, as was Gilbert the Bad in the stained-glass window,...
...sometimes altogether impalpable, like the image of Genevieve de Brabant, ancestress of the Guermantes family.
The castle's park...I dreamed that Madame de Guermantes had me come there, in love with me by a sudden caprice; every day she fished for trout there with me.
She would have me tell her the subject of poems that I intended to compose. And those dreams alerted me that, since I wanted to be a writer someday, it was time to figure out what I planned to write.
I felt that I had no talent...
...or maybe a brain fever was preventing it from coming to the fore.
So, discouraged, I renounced literature forever, despite the encouragement Bloch had given me.

One day my mother said to me:
YOU KNOW YOU'RE ALWAYS TALKING ABOUT MADAME DE GUERMANTES. SINCE SHE WAS DOCTOR PERCEPIED'S PATIENT FOUR YEARS AGO, SHE'S TO COME TO COMBRAY TO ATTEND THE MARRIAGE OF HIS DAUGHTER. YOU'LL BE ABLE TO SEE HER AT THE CEREMONY.
THAT'S IT, THAT'S ALL THERE IS TO MADAME DE GUERMANTES!
My disappointment was great. It came from me never having realized that, when I thought of Madame de Guermantes, I thought of her in the colors...
...of a tapestry...
...or of a stained-glass window,...
GVERMANT
VS
E
...in another century, of a different sort than the rest of living beings.

Never had I considered that she might have a red face or a mauve scarf like Madame Sazerat...
...that her body, ignorant of the name others gave to it, belonged to a certain feminine type that also included the wives of doctors and merchants.
But...my imagination, paralyzed for a moment upon contact with a reality so different than the one it had expected, began to react:
GLORIOUS EVEN BEFORE CHARLEMAGNE, THE GUERMANTES HAD THE RIGHT OF LIFE AND DEATH OVER THEIR VASSALS; THE DUCHESS OF GUERMANTES DESCENDS FROM GENEVIEVE DE BRABANT. SHE DOESN'T KNOW, NOR WOULD CONSENT TO MEET ANY OF THE PEOPLE HERE.
I see her again, especially at the moment of the recession from the sacristy.
THAT LADY IS MADAME DE GUERMANTES?
YES, MONSIEUR.
SHE'S BETTER LOOKING THAN MADAME SAZERAT.
...AND MLLE. VINTEUIL!
HOW BEAUTIFUL SHE IS! WHAT NOBILITY! SHE'S INDEED A PROUD GUERMANTES, THIS DESCENDANT OF GENEVIEVE DE BRABANT I HAVE BEFORE ME!
That smile fell upon me, who had never stopped looking at her.
!
I fancied that I pleased her.
And immediately, I loved her, for while it sometimes suffices for us to love a woman that she look at us with scorn, like I had thought Mademoiselle Swann had done, sometimes, too, it can be enough for her to look at us with kindness, as Madame de Guermantes was doing.

How often since that day, in my walks on the Guermantes' way, did it seem more distressing than ever before to not have any gift for writing, and to have to abandon ever being a famous writer!
Then suddenly, a rooftop, a reflection of sunlight on stone, the smell of a path would make me halt because of the singular pleasure they were giving me...
...and also because they seemed to be hiding something they invited one to come take.
I devoted myself to recalling exactly the line of the roof, the color of the stone, which, without my understanding why,...
...had seemed full to me, ready to open themselves, to deliver to me the contents of which they were nothing but a covering.
Once in the house, I would think of something else and thus many different images would pile up in my mind under which died long ago the presentient reality I never had the will to uncover.
Once however, when we had been fortunate enough to meet Doctor Percepied halfway home, who was passing by us in a carriage at full tilt, and who recognized us and had us climb aboard with him,...
CAN I GET IN FRONT, MAMA?
YES, IF YOU WISH.
...I got an impression of that sort and did not abandon it without deepening it a little.
I MUST STILL STOP AT A PATIENT'S IN MARTINVILLE-LE-SEC.

At a turn in the road, I suddenly felt that special pleasure alike no other at the first glimpse of the two steeples of Martinville, upon which the setting sun gleamed and which the movement of our carriage and bends in the road seemed to make change their position...
...then that of Vieuxvicq which, separated from them by a hill and a valley, and located on a higher plateau in the distance, still seemed very close to them.
GIDDY UP! ...GO!
AH, WE'RE COMING INTO MARTINVILLE!
...we stopped in front of Martinville's church. I got down to chat with my parents while awaiting the doctor...
...Then we got under way again...
YOU SEE, IT WASN'T TOO LONG!
The coachman did not seem inclined to talk..
...I was obliged, for lack of any other company, to make do...
...with that of my own and to try to remember my steeples.
Soon I had a thought that formed into words in my mind...
DOCTOR, COULD YOU GIVE ME A PENCIL AND SOME PAPER?
Without telling myself that whatever was concealed behind Martinville's steeples ought to be something analogous to a pretty phrase, I composed...

...in spite of the carriage's jolts...

...to relieve my conscience and to obey my enthusiasm, the short piece that follows...

...that I have since found again and to which I only had to make a few changes:

GEE UP! GO!...
ALONE, RISING ABOVE THE PLAIN'S LEVEL AS THOUGH LOST..."

"Alone, rising above the plain's level as though lost out in the country, the two steeples of Martinville climbed towards heaven.

Soon we saw three of them: coming to place itself opposite them with a hardy leap, a tardy steeple, that of Vieuxvicq, had joined them.

The minutes were passing by, we were going quickly and yet the three steeples were still far ahead of us, like three birds seated on the plain, immobile, that one distinguishes in the sunlight. Then the Vieuxvicq steeple pulled away, distancing itself, and the steeples of Martinville alone remained, lit by the beams of the setting sun which, even at this distance, I saw at play, smiling on their sloping sides.

We had been so long about getting closer to them that I was thinking of the time it would still take to reach them when, suddenly, the carriage having turned, it deposited us at their feet; and they had so rudely thrown themselves in front of the car, that we barely had time to stop to not crash into the steps.

We continued on our route; we had already left Martinville a short while since and the village, after having accompanied us for several seconds, had disappeared. Standing alone on the horizon watching us flee, its steeples and that of Vieuxvicq waved their sunlit summits as a gesture of farewell.

Sometimes, one would efface itself so that the other two might see us for an instant yet; but the road changed directions, they veered in the light like three golden pivots and disappeared before my eyes.

But, a little later, once we were already close to Combray, the sun having now set, I saw them one last time from afar; they were now only like three flowers painted on the sky above the low line of the fields.

They also made me think of the three girls in a legend, abandoned in a lonely place where darkness was already falling; and while we moved away at a gallop, I saw them shyly search for their path and after several clumsy stumbles of their noble silhouettes, press one against another, sliding one behind the other, forming, on the still-pink sky, but a single black form, charming and resigned, and fading away in the night."

I never thought again of that page, but at that moment, when I had finished writing it...
GEE UP! GIDDY UP!

...I found myself so happy, I felt that it had so perfectly cleared my mind of those steeples and all that they hid behind them, that, as if I were a hen and had just laid an egg, I started singing at the top of my voice.

Thus for me, do the Méséglise way and the Guermantes' way remain linked to so many small events of that one life of all the diverse lives that we lead on parallel lines, the one which is the fullest of events, the most rich in episodes, the life of the mind.
That scent of hawthorn collecting along the hedge, an echo-less sound of steps on the gravel of an alley, a bubble formed by the river water beside a water-plant and which immediately bursts...
...my exaltation carried them along and succeeded in making them traverse so many years, whereas, in turn, all around, the paths have been erased and all those who walked upon them and the memory of those who walked upon them are dead.
When on summer evenings, the harmonious sky rumbles like a wild beast and when everyone shuns the storm, it is to the Méséglise way that I owe it to remain alone in ecstacy...
...to breath in, through the noise of the falling rain, the odor of invisible...
...and persistant lilacs.

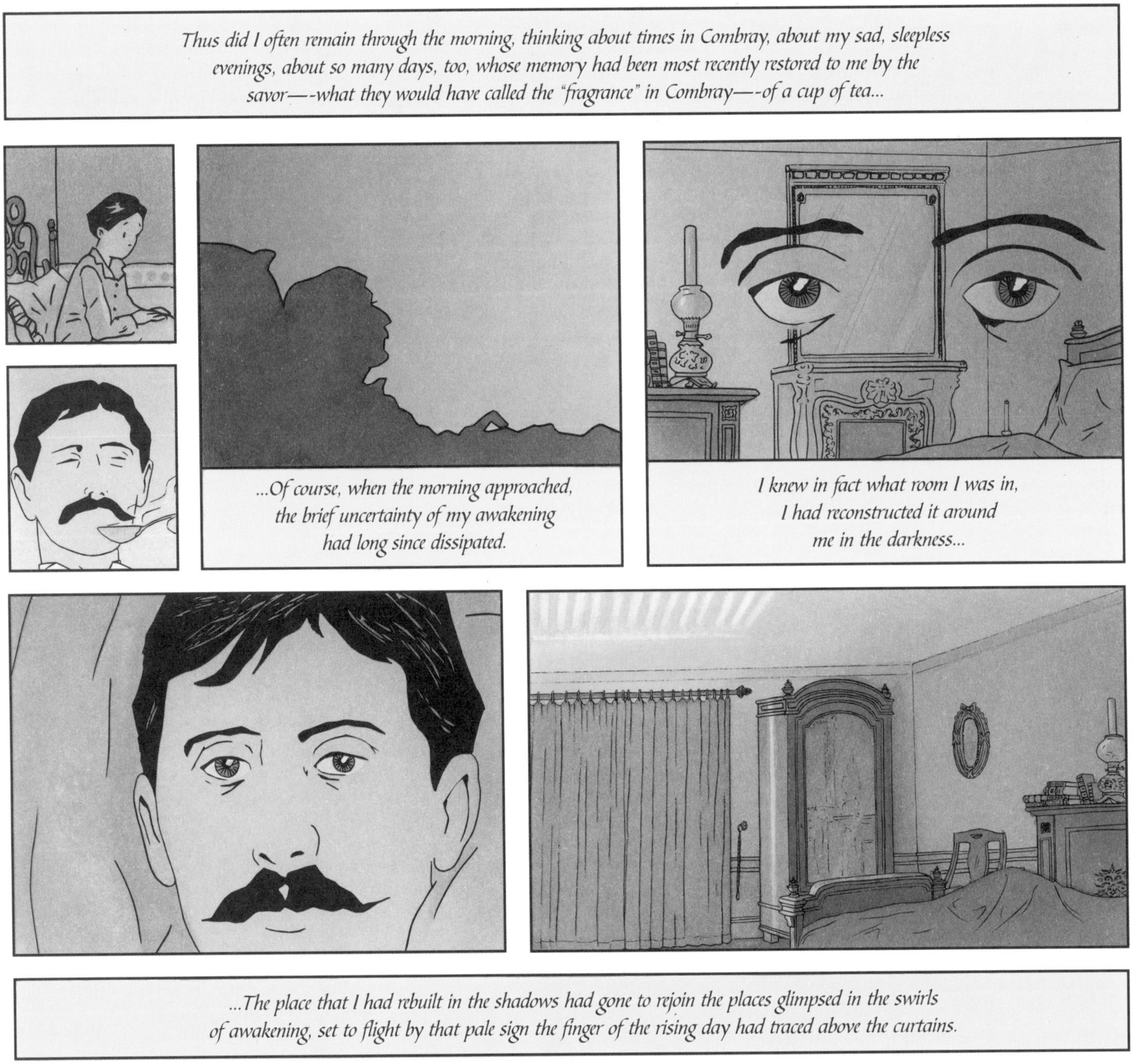
Thus did I often remain through the morning, thinking about times in Combray, about my sad, sleepless evenings, about so many days, too, whose memory had been most recently restored to me by the savor—-what they would have called the "fragrance" in Combray—-of a cup of tea...
...Of course, when the morning approached, the brief uncertainty of my awakening had long since dissipated.
I knew in fact what room I was in, I had reconstructed it around me in the darkness...
...The place that I had rebuilt in the shadows had gone to rejoin the places glimpsed in the swirls of awakening, set to flight by that pale sign the finger of the rising day had traced above the curtains.

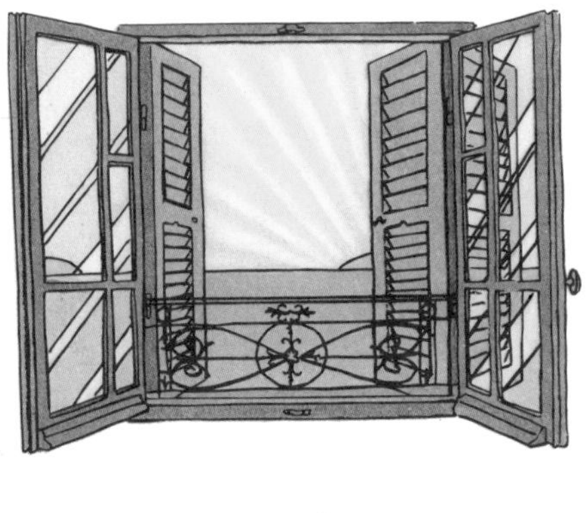

End of the first part